GUY STUFF
the BODY BOOK for BOYS

BY DR. CARA NATTERSON
ILLUSTRATED BY MICAH PLAYER

Published by American Girl Publishing

20 21 22 23 24 25 26 27 QP 18 17 16 15 14 13 12 11 10 9

Editorial Development: Mary Richards Beaumont, Barbara E. Stretchberry
Art Direction: Wendy Walsh Keogh
Production: Jeannette Bailey, Caryl Boyer, Cynthia Stiles, Kristi Tabrizi
Illustrations: Micah Player

This book is not intended to replace the advice of or treatment by other health-care
professionals. It should be considered an additional resource only. Questions and concerns about
mental or physical health should always be discussed with a doctor or other health-care professional.

Cataloging-in-Publication data available from the Library of Congress

? americangirl.com/service

Parents, request a FREE catalog at **americangirl.com/catalog**.
Sign up at **americangirl.com/email** to receive the latest news and exclusive offers.

LETTER to YOU...

Dear READER,

Are you ready for this thing called puberty?

No matter who you are, what you look like, or where you live, you will go through puberty. All kids do. Puberty is the word for all the body and mind changes that happen to everyone as they become teenagers and eventually, adults.

As you get older, your body will grow and transform and your brain will develop, too. Sometimes the changes in your body and mind will feel exciting, and sometimes they will feel awkward or embarrassing. You might have questions about what's happening or what's going to happen. This book is here to help you know what to expect as you get older.

We hope that the head-to-toe advice in this book will give you the words to start conversations with your parents or other adults you trust. Your parents were there for you when you were little, and they can be there for you now. Be sure to let them know how you're feeling and ask them all of your questions.

Take the time to learn more about yourself and the changes that are happening. You'll feel more confident about the boy you are and the young man you are becoming.

your FRIENDS at
GUY STUFF

CONTENTS

YOU only HAVE ONE BODY,

BODY BASICS 1

BUT BOY does it CHANGE.

HANDLING THIS IS all ABOUT...

EXPECTATIONS

HABITS and

ATTITUDE.

THE BASIC FACTS

That body you've got? It's going to change, and you're going to have to start taking care of it.

Get Ready for Some Changes

Your body is about to start growing and transforming *big-time*—or maybe this has already begun. All of it can feel awkward, uncomfortable, even gross. On the flip side, it's sort of awesome that you don't actually have to do any-thing—you can just sit back as your body transforms itself. But because it's all new and unfamiliar, you are guaranteed to have some questions about what's happening. Knowing the facts will help you take care of yourself better. It makes all of this changing seem less major.

Let's tackle the biggest question right now, before this book even really begins. **What is puberty?** It just means the process of growing and changing from a kid into an adult. Everybody goes through it—girls and guys. And every adult everywhere has gone through it, from parents to presidents, astronauts to athletes. So you are absolutely NOT alone in this.

The puberty time line:

Puberty starts for most boys between the ages of 9 and 14.

Puberty is finished when your body has reached its adult height, shape, and appearance. This usually means that you are in puberty throughout all of your teen years.

the BASIC FACTS. YOU WILL:

GROW TALLER

SPROUT HAIR

SWEAT MORE.

DEVELOP MUSCLES

SEE SOME CHANGES in SKIN TEXTURE

SEE CHANGES IN HAIR. COLOR TEXTURE AMOUNT *WAVVY MORE

GET A DEEPER VOICE

SEE CHANGES to YOUR PRIVATE PARTS

EXPERIENCE NEW EMOTIONS

All this stuff happens in a slightly different order for every guy. The unpredictability comes from the fact that these changes are caused by hormones, which are chemicals that your body produces to transform you, slowly, from a young boy into a man.

This book is not a substitute for talking to your parents, your doctor, or other adults you trust—people whose job it is to take care of you. No question is too silly or too embarrassing to ask. Remember, the grown-ups in your life were once your age, too, and have experience and wisdom to share with you.

GOOD HABITS

This stuff works now—and later. You'll use this advice forever, so . . . you're welcome.

The "Rules"

Everything in this book that teaches you how to take care of yourself is as true for a kid as it is for an adult. Yep, that's right—the "rules" here apply to you, your parents, and your grandparents, too. The info you will learn about nutrition and exercise and sleep and keeping clean is true for pretty much everyone. These are skills that you will use for the rest of your life.

We all forget to do these things sometimes—that's not a huge deal. The most important thing is to get into healthy habits now so that you're in a good routine by the time your body has gone through these big changes. Besides, habits are a lot easier to remember than rules. Take all of this information and turn it into stuff you do automatically. Then you are set up for a healthy life.

Here are the most important basics when it comes to taking care of your body. There's lots more info in the pages to come, but for those of you who like to think big, these are the five main ideas:

1. Pay attention:

That means get better at listening to your body. Try to recognize feelings such as being thirsty or hungry or tired. Start thinking about how your moods and choices affect others. It's hard to make smart choices when you aren't recognizing what's going on with you in the first place.

4. Sleep:

Getting a good night's sleep every night might just be the most important health tip anyone will ever give you!

2. Exercise and eat well:

You've heard this a thousand times, but eat healthy foods and get moving every day. Seriously, spending a little less time on screens and paying a little more attention to what you put into your mouth will probably make you feel amazing.

5. Keep clean:

It keeps you healthy, and it makes you feel—and smell!—better, too. Besides, stink tends to drive people away.

3. Ask questions:

If you aren't sure about something, ask someone who knows. There's nothing wrong with not knowing—this is all new stuff. And if you have a question, you can bet someone else wonders the same thing, too. Go to a person, though—a trusted adult—NOT a computer. You need good information, and random websites don't always provide that.

Take Control

During puberty, it's a sure thing that you are going to have moments when you feel like your body is totally rebelling against you. Sometimes you just have to ride it out. But a lot of the time, you can take control over the situation by treating your body with respect.

Put good stuff in it: Eat healthy food and drink lots of water.
Put good stuff on it: Wear helmets, sunscreen, and hats when needed.
Put it to bed: Get enough sleep to reboot for the next day.

Growing up healthfully is as much about what you *don't* do to your body as it is about what you *do* do. So keep the bad stuff out.

PRIVACY

Your body belongs to you. That means you get to make the call about how you share your personal space with others (and, by the way, others get to make the same call about themselves).

Some kids are more touchy-feely than others, but in general there are good kinds of touching and not-good kinds. The good touch is a hug from your grandma. The not-good one is contact from a stranger—or even from someone you know—that feels awkward or uncomfortable. If anyone ever touches you this way, tell them it's not OK. If he or she tells you to keep it a secret, DON'T. Tell a trusted adult right away.

Future You

Want to know what you are going to look like when you're all grown up? Yeah, so does everyone else your age. Sorry—there is no way to predict exactly how tall you will be or how muscular or how hairy. There are some clues, though.

Your **genes** are the microscopic instruction manuals that tell your body how to grow and develop. They determine qualities such as your height, eye color, and skin tone. Genes affect the organs inside your body, too. They even play a role in your personality.

You don't have any control over your genes—you have inherited these from your biological parents. But you do have tons of control over how you treat your body, and, believe it or not, this affects the way your genes work. For instance, your genes might be programmed to make you really tall, but if you don't eat and sleep well, then you won't get there. So on one hand, puberty is something that just *happens* to you. On the other hand, there are many times when you are still in charge.

MAGNIFIED MANY MANY TIMES and IT'S ALSO POSSIBLE that GENES DON'T LOOK LIKE JELLY BEANS WITH FACES.

Genes also determine *when* you go through puberty. It can feel super awkward to be the very first or very last to change. But it will happen when the time is right for you—and when your genes say so. So don't compare yourself to others. Puberty isn't a race.

EARLY BLOOMERS vs. LATE BLOOMERS

An **early bloomer** is someone who enters puberty on the younger side. That person might look old for his age—he might be taller or hairier than other kids in his class, at least at first. But after a while, other kids will catch up, and many may actually pass him. Just because a kid starts developing young doesn't mean he's going to be the biggest and strongest. Here's another thing: when early bloomers look much older than they really are, adults might assume they are also more mature. This is usually not the case, and it can put early bloomers in situations they aren't ready for.

A **late bloomer** is the opposite: one of the last to start puberty. These kids often look younger than they actually are—a fact that can be super annoying when adults treat them like little kids. Late bloomers grow after many of their classmates, so they tend to be shorter than everyone . . . at least for a while. It's good to know that even though a kid might go through puberty on the later end, it doesn't mean that he will end up small.

ATTITUDE

Sometimes it's hard to figure out how to act. You're not alone—everyone your age is going through that.

Attitude Is Everything

While you are going through puberty, it's totally normal to doubt yourself or question how others see you. But here's a fact that might change the way you see yourself: Having a *positive attitude* often makes others want to be around you. It's true—feeling good about yourself actually makes you more attractive and appealing to others.

The opposite is true, too. If you have a *negative attitude*, it pushes people away. Be careful, though, because if you are too confident, people will think you are arrogant or annoying and won't want to hang around you at all.

Let It Out

Don't keep all these emotions to yourself. Seriously!

It's not always easy to feel confident. During those times when you have doubts, it makes a huge difference to talk it out with a parent, a trusted adult, or a close friend who has got your back. Vent about the stuff that is getting you down so that those emotions don't build up inside. You know what happens when you shake a soda can and then open it? Yeah, the soda explodes out. That's what can happen when you hold down your feelings for too long. And when you finally let them out, things can get messy.

Don't forget to talk out the good stuff, too. Share when you've had a huge win. Let other people laugh with you and celebrate you. Remember: Communication doesn't only have to be about negative stuff.

I MEAN, I JUST SLEPT and SLEPT. AND I HAD the MOST AMAZING DREAMS. I AM SOOOO GOOD at THIS HIBERNATION THING. I MEAN, LIKE REALLY GOOD...

BE CONFIDENT (not BRAGGY)

It's a fine line. Confidence is good, but too much can be a turnoff.

Confident guys
- Speak with certainty and look the other person directly in the eye.
- Remember to ask questions of the other person in the conversation.
- Don't yell or speak over other people.
- Don't list all the great things they have done.

Arrogant guys
- Boast about their accomplishments.
- Often forget to ask about other people.
- Love to talk about themselves and tend to need the last word.
- Sometimes speak with a too-loud voice.

ALL THE FEELS

HAIR CARE

The big news is that mostly you just need to keep it clean.

Wash Up

As you get older, your hair will probably change. It might get oilier, curlier, or darker. All normal. Keep your hair clean by washing it regularly using two things: shampoo and water. Don't use body wash on your hair unless the bottle specifically says it's also a shampoo. How often you wash depends on the type of hair you have and how sweaty or stinky you happen to be from one day to the next.

LONG LOCKS

For you guys with longer hair that tangles, try using conditioner after you shampoo. And if you've got dry and delicate hair, you might choose a leave-in conditioning treatment.

HEADS UP!

'Do It

How annoying is it when adults constantly ask you to fix your hair? There's a reason they do that, though—you look more ready for the world when you are cleaned up, and having neat hair is part of that. No matter your hairstyle, it's important to make an effort to look pulled together.

- **Short Hair?** Brush or comb it while it is still damp.

- **Longer Hair?** You'll probably need to brush it a little more or it will tangle. If you hit a knot, just work through it gently—don't yank.

- **Curly Hair?** You may be a guy who does best with a finger brush—yep, you just run your fingers through your clean, damp hair.

- **Textured or Natural Hair?** You might need a detangling brush to work out knots in your damp hair, and then use a wire comb or your hands to shape your style.

- **Buzz Cut?** OK, you probably get out of styling.

Hair Products

A little goes a long way! If you are into gel or styling creams, apply a small amount—about the size of a pea—to your hands first, rub your hands together for a sec, and then work the product through your hair. If you put large gobs straight onto your head, you may wind up with sticky chunks of hair or dusty flakes from the excess product.

STYLE!

STYLES

You might think a particular hairstyle looks awesome, but your mom or dad totally disagrees. What to do about it? Try talking. Explain what you like and why you like it. You may be able to convince them—or at least find a compromise.

ACTUAL SIZE

HAIR SCARES

Here's what to do when hair-raising horrors happen.

Problem: Oily-looking hair, especially near the scalp

Why? During puberty, oil glands get more active. This extra oil in the scalp makes hair greasy.

Solution: Change how often you shampoo. You probably will need to do it more frequently, but all heads are different.

Don't ignore it and think it'll just go away.

Problem: White flaky stuff in your hair or on the shoulders of your shirt

Why? You have dry skin in your scalp, which gets itchy and flaky. Or you have used too much product, which turns white and flaky in your hair, imitating actual dandruff.

Solution: You can try using a dandruff shampoo, and definitely use less styling product. If it doesn't get better, ask your doctor for suggestions.

Don't keep using products that seem to make the problem worse.

Problem: A super-itchy head, and, when an adult checks, there are tiny bugs or teeny eggs in your hair

Why? Lice are teeny, gray, wingless parasites that live on strands of human hair. They don't jump or fly, but they do climb up the hair shaft and bite the scalp, leaving tiny sores that itch like crazy.

Solution: You'll need to get help combing out your hair using a special comb to remove all the lice and their eggs. You might also need a special shampoo or hair treatment.

Don't share combs, brushes, hats, or head-phones. And don't put your head right next to someone else's when taking a selfie or looking at the same small screen. These are easy ways to get—or give—lice.

DEALING with LICE

If you think you've got lice, ask your doctor or school nurse to check. They know a louse when they see one. If it turns out that you do have lice, it doesn't mean you are dirty—in fact, lice like clean heads. Getting rid of them isn't hard, but it takes lots of patience. A parent can buy special products at the drugstore and follow the instructions, including combing out your hair very carefully using a special comb to get rid of the lice and keep them from coming back.

HEADS UP!

EARS

Listen, ears are pretty easy. They just need a little help from you to stay clean and healthy and do their job.

Other super-loud noises can cause hearing problems, like lawnmowers, power tools, and giant concert speakers blasting music. If you are around these, try earplugs. But you don't need to wear earplugs when your parents are reminding you to clean up your room!

Keeping 'Em Clean

When you shower, you actually wash your ears when the water and shampoo run down your head. That's enough.

Do shake your head like a dog to get the excess water out, and then wipe the outer part of your ears with a towel.

Don't stick anything into your ears—not even a cotton swab. You could do serious damage to your eardrums or ear canals.

What's Wax?

That sticky yellowish gunk inside your ears is supposed to be there—it traps dirt. Some people have too much wax, and sometimes this can make it hard to hear. If your ears feel plugged, talk to your doctor to find a safe way to remove it.

Pierced Ears

Thinking about ear piercing?

First stop: A parent! You MUST have an official OK.

Next stop: A professional who uses clean, sterile equipment.

The long haul: It takes two to three months for the holes to heal before you can change an earring. And newly pierced ears need to be cleaned daily. If the area is ever red, crusty, tender, or itchy, it might be infected. Show it to an adult.

Headphones and Earbuds

Sometimes there's nothing better than turning on music and tuning out the world. But be careful about how high you turn up the volume. Over time, loud noises can damage hearing. If you are wearing earbuds or headphones and a person standing next to you can hear your music easily, then the volume is too loud. Turn it down!

HEADS UP!

SWIMMER'S EAR

When bacteria and moisture mix in your ear canal, the result is a really painful earache that hurts especially when you pull on the ear. The most likely time for this to happen? When you are doing lots of swimming.

What to do about it: With a parent, try a home remedy. Mix 1 teaspoon rubbing alcohol and 1 teaspoon white vinegar. Tilt your head so that the painful ear is pointed toward the sky. A parent can put one drop of the mixture in your ear (use a clean pinky finger and just let it drip down). Wait a few seconds before turning your head straight again.

What if it's not getting better or it's a lot worse? See your doctor.

How to prevent it: If you get swimmer's ear regularly, your parent can use a drop of the alcohol and vinegar mixture in your ear after swimming. But be sure to towel-dry your ear first.

Note: Swimmer's ear is different from a middle-ear infection. Not sure which you have? Let a doctor check it out!

HEADS UP!

23

EYES

Look, you need to take care of your eyes! See?

Glasses

Not sure if you need glasses? Here are some clues that you might:
- You have trouble reading or seeing what's written on the board at school.
- You get headaches while reading or right after you have finished.
- Objects often look blurry either at a distance or up close.
- You see double (but not when you are crossing your eyes!).

Eye Exams

Even if you aren't having difficulty with your vision, your eyes need to be checked just like every other part of your body—it's important to make sure that they're healthy, even if you're seeing well. Some people get this done at their regular doctor checkup, while others go to a special eye doctor. All you do is read a few charts. And then your eyes will be checked with a tool called an ophthalmoscope, which can see all the way to the back of your eyeball. If you are seeing an eye doctor, you may have a few more vision games, like trying to see flashing lights in the corner of the room or looking at screens through cool machine lenses.

You're Not Alone

Your eyes change as you grow. That's why some kids need glasses early but outgrow them by the time they are teenagers or adults. Other kids might have perfect vision until they are older, and then they suddenly need some help seeing things. These days, wearing glasses is pretty cool.

Eyewear

Glasses come in a ton of colors and styles. They don't just change how you see but also how you look. **Contact lenses** go right on top of the eyeball, changing the way you see without anyone noticing. But contacts require a lot more care than glasses because you have to change or clean them daily.

Eye Protection

Everyone should wear sunglasses, regardless of how well they can see. That's because the eyes can burn just like the skin. Look for shades marked "UVA/UVB protection," a must for protecting your eyes in the sun. You also could shop for shades with polarized lenses, which are designed to reduce the sun's glare. If you wear glasses for vision, you can get a pair that turns darker when you go outside—these "transitional" lenses turn your glasses into sunglasses automatically.

Don't Fry Your Eye

Seriously, don't stare into bright lights. If you shine a flashlight into your eyes or stare at the sun, you'll have a lot of trouble seeing for the next few minutes. This is not a funny trick—you can do real damage by burning your eye. Along the same lines, never look directly at a solar eclipse, even with sunglasses.

MOUTH

Keep your teeth bright and your breath all right
with these brushing basics.

Toothbrush Tips

All you need to know about picking a toothbrush:

- Get one with a small head and SOFT bristles. Hard ones can hurt
  your gums.
- Battery-operated or rechargeable toothbrushes vibrate, helping to
  maximize the clean.
- Remember: Toothbrushes (or electric toothbrush heads) are disposable
  and need to be changed every two to three months, or even sooner if
  the bristles get frayed. Toss a toothbrush after you have been sick, and
  start fresh with
  a clean one.

Healthy Gums

Your gums need just as much attention as your teeth. If you
ignore them, they can get red, swollen, and painful. That's called
gingivitis. This is easy to prevent, though. Just floss at least once
a day to get rid of food stuck between your teeth and gums.
Dental floss comes in lots of sizes, textures, and flavors, so try
different kinds to see which you like best.

Why Brush?

Brushing is key if you want to look and smell good. Plus, it helps prevent cavities, which happen when you don't brush plaque off your teeth. **Plaque** is a film containing bacteria and sugars, and it is linked to cavities and gum disease. When plaque is visible, it looks gross, too. Attack the plaque by brushing your teeth first thing in the morning and again at bedtime for two minutes each time—not two seconds! Some people brush after eating, too.

HOW to BRUSH

1. Prep your toothbrush with toothpaste. Remember, a little is all you need—a glob about the size of a large pea is usually plenty to get the job done.

2. Hold your toothbrush at an angle to your gum line. Brush back and forth in small strokes or in tiny circles, one tooth at a time. Repeat until you've scrubbed every single tooth.

3. Now do the back side of each tooth, using the same back-and-forth or circular motion and going right up to the gum line. Use the tip of the brush to get behind your front teeth. Don't forget the surface of your molars.

4. Brush your tongue, too! Otherwise, your breath will still stink. So that's why proper brushing takes two full minutes!

HEADS UP!

27

HOW to FLOSS

There are really two ways to do this:

1. The first way is to use a flosser that holds floss in place and makes it easier for you to reach the back corners of your mouth.

CLOSE-UP!

2. Or use your fingers as the flosser: Pull a strand of floss about a foot long and wind each end of the floss around a finger from each hand (most people use the index or middle fingers), leaving a short section of string in between. Put a little extra pressure on the floss with your thumbs, and pull your hands apart so the string is tight. You are ready to go.

3. No matter how you hold the floss, your job is to gently guide the floss between two of your teeth, wiggling it all the way up to the gum line and down the sides. Floss between each pair of teeth, and don't forget to floss at the very end of each row, behind the back teeth.

Why Floss?

If you've ever gotten a whiff of stinky breath—*yikes!*—it's something you definitely want to avoid. Bad breath (doctors call it **halitosis**) can be caused by all sorts of things, but most often it's a sign that you're not brushing and flossing well. When food is stuck between your teeth, it can start to stink, sort of like garbage sitting in a garbage can. Only flossing can get that stench out.

If you are brushing and flossing well and your mouth still reeks, have a doctor check you out. Infections in the nose and throat can create mega-smells as well.

WHY?

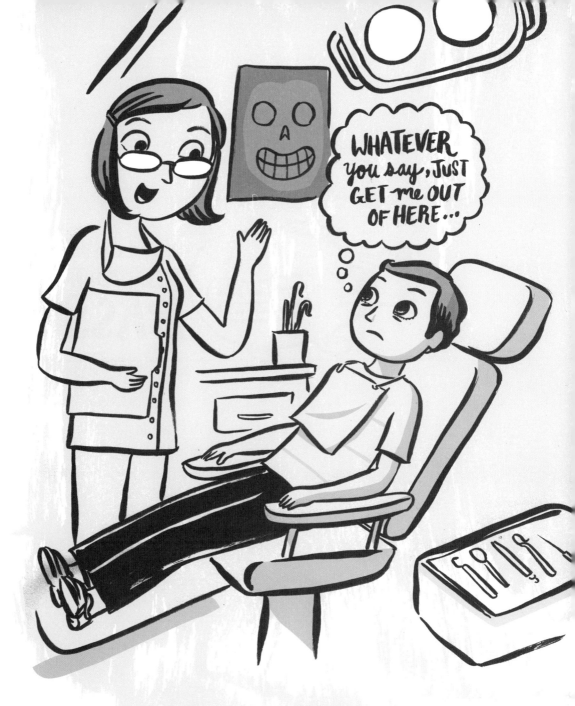

Regular Visits

Some people get really stressed out about visiting the dentist or ortho-dontist (the specialist who puts on braces to straighten teeth). Some tips to help you chill out:

- Know what to expect: Ask your doctor to explain what will happen before the exam begins.
- Take care to prepare: The better you take care of your teeth, the easier the visit will be. Habits such as daily brushing and flossing, healthy eating, and regular checkups are the best way to avoid cavities and other problems that require the dentist to spend more time in your mouth.
- Remember that it's good for you: Your teeth need to last a lifetime. Taking care of them includes these types of visits.

BRACES

Lots of people get braces. Might as well show yours off!

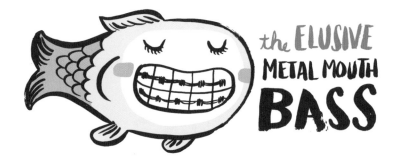

the ELUSIVE METAL MOUTH BASS

Getting Braces

Millions of people, both kids and adults, have mouths full of metal. It isn't forever! Braces, expanders, retainers, spacers, bite guards, and other appliances will come off one day, leaving you with nicely straightened teeth. If you do end up needing orthodontic treatment, you'll need to change certain habits for a while.

Brushing with Hardware

When you've got hardware in your mouth, brushing your teeth is more important than ever because food can get trapped in the wires and brackets. That food causes plaque buildup and stinky breath. To fight back:

- Try to brush after every meal.
- At least once a day, spend a good amount of time cleaning in between teeth and wires or brackets.
- If your doctor recommends special equipment such as an electric toothbrush or a water squirter that helps to rinse the hard-to-reach areas, give it a try.

THIS IS MY LIFE NOW.

Flossing with Hardware

Flossing when you have a wire in the way takes extra time and patience. But it's key for better mouth health and far better breath. Most people floss at night because that's when they have the time. Your dentist or orthodontist will show you how to floss around your wires the first couple of times, but then you'll be good to go.

HEADS UP!

no

CHIPS

CARAMELS

GUMMIES

PHEW!

STICKY CANDY

CHEWING
ICE CUBES

CORN ON THE COB

Off-Limits

Having hardware in your mouth restricts what you can eat. That's because hard foods can break the orthodonture, and sticky foods will get, well, stuck in it. Saying no to this stuff can be hard, but it's much easier than having to constantly visit the orthodontist get your hardware fixed. Here are some things to remember:

• Some foods, such as apples, can be cut into bite-size bits.
• Other foods need to be cut out entirely, particularly gooey, chewy, sticky snacks such as caramels and gummies that stick to the teeth long after you are done eating.
• Chewing ice cubes can break braces or wires, so avoid those, too.

FACE

Taking care of the skin on your face is easy—just wash it!

FACE PRODUCTS

Face-care products are not just for girls, even though they are often advertised this way. If you skip that whole section of the store, you and your face are missing out. Remember that guys need sunscreen, moisturizer, and lip balm, too.

Seriously, Wash Your Face

If you've got a face, you have to wash it. You need to do this thoroughly at least once a day, usually at bedtime. It's really not a big deal—at most, it takes 30 seconds of your day. Here's how:

1. Choose a mild soap or cleanser that's formulated for your face.
2. Lather up.
3. Wash with your hands or a soft, clean washcloth and warm (not super hot) water.
4. Rinse your skin well to remove the soap and pat dry.

During the other times of the day when you think you might have food or dirt on your face, just wipe it off. Ignoring it doesn't make it disappear, and even though you may not have to see all that junk on your face, everyone else does.

Chapped Lips

When lips are chapped, it means they are too dry. Here's how to fix the problem:

• Use a lip balm or ointment to moisturize. When you are outside, choose a balm with sunscreen in it.
• Make sure you're drinking enough water—this will help to hydrate dry, cracked lips.
• Try not to lick your lips when they feel dry. That makes the dryness worse, because even though you feel like you are "moisturizing" your lips with saliva, the air quickly dries them, leading to more chapping and even cracking. *Ouch.*

HEADS UP!

Ring Around Your Lips

Do you have a bright red circle around your lips? Does it sting or itch? That's chapped skin and, whether or not you realize it, you are probably licking the skin to make it feel less irritated. The problem is that licking just wets the skin, then the skin dries and gets even more irritated. Eventually bacteria can grow there, too, turning the ring from pinkish to bright red. The only way to make the redness disappear is to stop licking, which can be super hard. Lip balms that moisturize your skin without irritating it can help a lot—plus, they make it much less likely that you will keep licking the area.

The Skin You're In

The skin on your face is different from the skin on other parts of your body: It's thinner, more sensitive, and exposed to a whole lot more sun and wind. This means that you need to use products that won't irritate it. The best ones say "for the face" on the label and are **hypoallergenic,** which means free of irritating ingredients.

If your skin is . . .	Use a product that is . . .	You can try this trick, too . . .
oily or pimply	**oil-free** 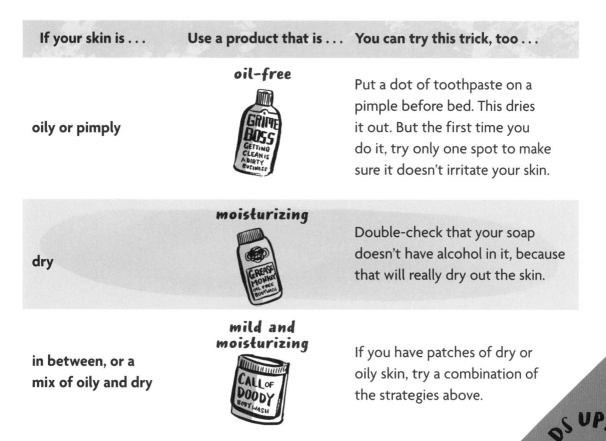 GRIME BOSS GETTING CLEAN IS A DIRTY BUSINESS	Put a dot of toothpaste on a pimple before bed. This dries it out. But the first time you do it, try only one spot to make sure it doesn't irritate your skin.
dry	**moisturizing** GREASE MONKEY OIL-FREE BODYWASH	Double-check that your soap doesn't have alcohol in it, because that will really dry out the skin.
in between, or a mix of oily and dry	**mild and moisturizing** CALL OF DOODY BODYWASH	If you have patches of dry or oily skin, try a combination of the strategies above.

Almost everybody deals with face flare-ups at some point. But you can learn to fight back!

Why You Have Zits

Acne. Zits. Pimples. Breakouts. Thanks to puberty, your body has started to produce more oil.

OIL + BACTERIA + DEAD SKIN CELLS = CLOGGED PORES...
and VOILA! YOU HAVE a PIMPLE. YAY!

Pretty much every kid you know will have acne at some point. Some people get just a few zits here and there, while others might have it on their faces, chests, and backs. How many zits you will have and where you will have them mainly depends on your genetics.

Blackhead: a pimple that looks like it has a black dot in the middle. That dot is NOT made from dirt but rather from pigment cells—the cells that determine your skin color.

Whitehead: a pimple that looks white in the middle. That white stuff is made from the cells in your body that are designed to fight infection.

Scab: the crusty stuff covering a picked or popped zit. Your body is trying to heal and makes this cap to protect itself. It's the exact same thing that happens when you get a cut anywhere else on your skin.

Pore: a natural hole in your skin where oils are released. You have thousands of pores. During puberty, they make more oil, get clogged with old skin cells, and trap bacteria. All this can cause a mini-infection that shows up as a pimple.

Zits are annoying. They can be embarrassing. They are usually not the look you are going for. But having zits does not mean that someone is dirty. Lots of kids work really hard to keep their skin clean, and they still get zits. Remember, pimples come from having extra oil on the skin and clogged pores. Yes, a clean face helps, but unfortunately, it doesn't always solve the problem.

STRIKING BACK

No one can avoid zits entirely, but you can take some steps to minimize them.

Keep your face clean. Wash daily with a mild soap or cleanser. Don't overdo it—harsh scrubbing and rubbing can actually make things worse.

Don't pick at or pop pimples. When you do, the zit gets irritated and goes from being a small bump to a much larger, redder, more obvious one. Plus, the oils and dirt on your fingers make the whole situation worse. And the worst part is that picking a pimple can cause a permanent scar.

You can use products to treat pimples. These dry out the zit so that it goes away more quickly. But some zit-relievers have ingredients that can actually make the skin worse!

Products that contain rubbing alcohol can over-dry the skin. They might clear up a breakout one day but double it the next.

Added perfumes and colors in skin-care products can irritate the skin, causing redness, so try to use products without them.

The best products usually contain ingredients such as retinols or benzoyl peroxide that help to reduce oil and get rid of dead skin cells.

Talk to your doctor. Out-of-control acne may call for medical attention. Your doctor can prescribe special creams or pills that are stronger than regular products.

Sunny day? Snowy day? The sun doesn't care.
Take steps to block its rays.

REAPPLY

Sunscreen wears off. By the afternoon, it won't work if you put it on first thing in the morning. You actually need to reapply sunscreen every two to four hours—and more frequently if you are swimming.

Protect Your Skin

The sun's rays are intense, even when the sky is cloudy. Rays do the most damage to our skin in the middle of the day, between about 10 a.m. and 3 p.m. And rays don't just come out of the sky. At the beach, the sand and water reflect the sun's rays. By the pool, sunlight bounces off the water—and onto you. Skiing or snowboarding? Snow reflects sunlight, too. It's pretty easy to protect yourself, though. No matter what color skin you have, do a few things that take only a moment of your day:

Slather on: Apply sunscreen before leaving the house in the morning. Don't forget to put it everywhere that is exposed to sunlight, including around your shirt neckline and your ears.

Check SPF: Use a sunscreen with a sun protection factor (or SPF) of 30–50. The higher the SPF, the better the protection. Choose sunscreen that offers both UVA and UVB protection.

Swim safely: Going swimming? Wear water-resistant sunscreen, and put it on at least 15 minutes before getting wet. Reapply after you dry off.

Grab a hat: And sunglasses. And a shirt. Yeah, just like parents always tell you. These items all provide great protection for your skin. They also make it more comfortable to be out in the bright, hot sun.

Sun Safety

All types of skin can burn. Sunburns hurt when they happen, and they cause long-term damage to your skin. Burns that are followed by blistering and/or peeling are particularly unhealthy. Protecting your skin with sunscreen, sun protective clothing, and shade helps prevent burns. Tanning isn't great for you, either, by the way. People who spend time in tanning salons when they are young have a much higher risk of skin cancers, even if they never burn.

Crazy Sun Fact

Your butt doesn't wrinkle! It develops skin folds as you get older, but no fine lines like on the face. That's because it pretty much never sees the sun.

how to HAVE HEALTHY HANDS

3

REACH!

and ODORLESS ARMPITS

...PLUS UNDERSTANDING NORMAL CHEST CHANGES.

REACH!

HANDS

Your hands matter—they do a lot of hard work!
So take care of them.

- **Hold a small object** such as a stone, ball, or even play putty to keep your hands busy and out of your mouth.

- **Coat your nails** with a special nail-biter's polish (it tastes really bad) to remind you to keep your fingers out of your mouth.

- **Put adhesive bandages** over your nails—or even wear gloves to bed!—so that you won't stick your fingers in your mouth while you're sleeping.

- **Set goals** and keep track of how many days you go without giving in to your habit. This works especially well if you reward yourself at the end.

- If all else fails, **talk to a doctor** or dentist for ideas. But don't give up—it takes time and patience to undo habits you've had for years.

Wash Your Hands!

Your hands touch things constantly—doorknobs, pencils, desks, walls, countertops—and then you use those same hands to pick up food and eat it. The germs go right into your mouth. (By the way, those germs also go into your nose when you pick it and your eyes when you rub them!)

So wash your hands! Do it before eating, after going to the bathroom, if you have a cold (especially one with sneezing or nose-blowing), or anytime you stick your fingers into something gross or sticky. The best way to clean your hands is with soap and water. Yes, you can use an alcohol-based hand sanitizer, but 20 seconds of lathering with soap and rinsing under the tap is the best approach.

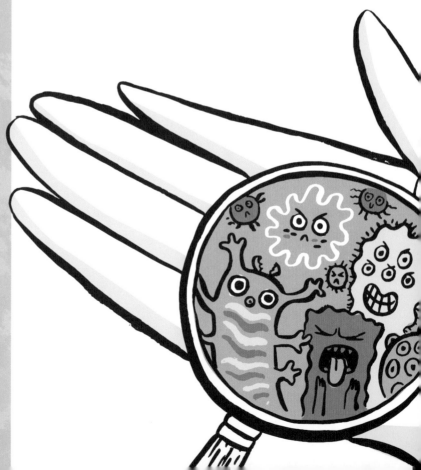

REACH!

Nailed It

Bitten and picked nails look pretty bad—they are often jagged along the edge, and they can have scabs where the broken skin has started to bleed. Plus, picked spots can get infected or just hurt like crazy.

Warts

These harmless little white or pinkish bumps of flesh are caused by a virus. They will go away on their own after a long time—it can take a year or more. If you don't want to wait, you can ask a parent to help you try a wart-removing product. Or try this trick: Put a piece of duct tape over the wart, and leave it on for five or six days. Remove the tape for a day to let the skin air out, and then reapply new tape for another five or six days. After a few rounds, your wart should be gone.

Calluses

These hard, rough patches of skin are caused by friction. Your body grows a layer of tough skin to protect the areas—such as your hands and feet—that get rubbed thanks to activities such as playing sports, raking leaves, or gripping the handlebars of your bike as you ride. Wear gloves to help prevent calluses.

Got dirty fingernails? Scrub your nails with a soft-bristled nailbrush to remove the dirt trapped underneath, and trim your nails with clippers so that they don't get too long. Longer nails trap dirt better than shorter ones.

A hangnail isn't really a nail—it's a painful split in the skin next to the nail (that skin is called the **cuticle**). Don't bite or rip the skin because it will hurt even more! Instead, clip the hanging skin as closely as possible to the finger, and then leave it alone. Picking at it will only make it feel worse.

Sharp edges? No problem. Use a nail file to round off any sharp corners or ragged edges.

UNDERARMS

Have you ever, EVER thought about your armpits?
Maybe not. But now that you're getting
older, you'll need to.

ABOUT AEROSOLS

Products that can be sprayed—also known as aerosols—can be convenient. But they can be irritating, too (for your nose and lungs, that is). Say that you spray an antiperspirant onto your armpit. Sure, some goes where you mean for it to, but you can also see the mist floating in the air around you. That means that you're breathing in what you're spraying on. This isn't good for anyone, especially people with allergies or asthma. And some aerosols aren't healthy for the environment, either. So if you have a choice, it's best to pick the nonspray version, whether it's hair product, sunscreen, or antiperspirant.

BO Is the Pits!

Sweating is the body's way of cooling down. When you are overheated, nothing cools you faster than sweating and then air-drying. During puberty, people start sweating more and in different places, including in the armpits. When all this extra sweat mixes with bacteria on your skin, it can produce a gnarly smell. That's body odor, or BO. This is pretty easy to fix, though: If you wash your armpits using lots of soap every time you shower or bathe, you will wash those bacteria off your skin and rinse away the stench.

Deodorants and Antiperspirants

You need more than just a shower to keep sweat and odor away. That's where antiperspirants and deodorants work their magic. Antiperspirants reduce sweating ("anti" = against; "perspire" = sweat). Deodorants deodorize, getting rid of nasty smells. Some products are a combination of antiperspirant and deodorant. They come in roll-ons, solid sticks, gels, and sprays. Pick the one that works best for you.

UNDERARM HAIR

Eventually, everyone gets hair under their arms. Underarm hair can show up almost anytime during puberty—generally between ages 11 and 17. Unlike many girls who shave their armpits, most boys leave the hair in place.

REACH!

STINK

Something smells . . . and it might be you! Totally normal and usually fixable, but it requires some effort.

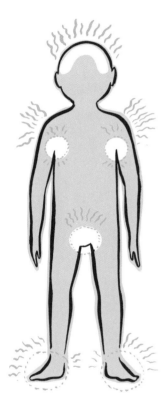

All-Over Stink

Your smell won't just radiate from your armpits, you know. Thanks to puberty, you might have stink creeping out from all corners of your body. The areas that get dark, hot, and sweaty are the first to reek: This includes armpits but also your groin and your feet, particularly in between your toes. Other parts can smell, too, like a greasy scalp or dirty ears. The craziest thing about body odor is that the person who has it doesn't always realize it—smelling yourself is tougher than you might think.

Hide the Stench?

So you think you can cover up one smell with another? Good luck! Trying to hide body odor with heavily scented body washes and colognes will usually make your stench worse, not better. It's like putting a bunch of roses on top of a trash pile. Does not help.

Clothes That Reek

Some athletic wear can start to smell even worse than your body. That's because some fabrics absorb both sweat and the bacteria from your skin. Once the bacteria—and their accompanying odor—get into the clothing, it's really hard to get out, even with regular washing. So before you pull on a shirt, sniff it. If you get a whiff of something gross, that smell will only get worse as you wear it throughout the day. Don't wear it! Put it back in the laundry and ask a parent to help you research techniques for washing bad odors out of sports clothing. If the stench is really intense or won't wash away, it may be time to toss the item altogether.

CHEST

Your upper body is gonna look different.
(Not just talking chest hair!)

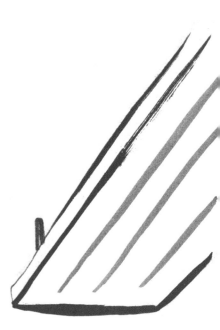

Wait, Those Aren't . . . Are They?!

All people—male and female—have breast tissue. The tissue doesn't turn into "real" breasts in most males. But because it is in your body, when you are going through puberty and all those hormones are flying around inside you, the breast tissue might begin to grow a little bit. You might see a small mound on one or both sides of your chest or feel some tenderness under your nipple. Scientists call it **gynecomastia,** and some of them estimate that it happens to half of all boys, maybe even more.

This is something that can really embarrass some guys, but it doesn't have to. It's just a fact of life.

The good news: It usually goes away on its own. You just have to be patient. And most of the time no one other than you notices it.

The bad news: For the boys who have it and really don't like it, their self-esteem can fall.

Can you avoid it? Maybe. For some guys, if it's gonna happen, it's gonna happen, and it's natural. Other guys carry around extra body weight that can give the appearance of gynecomastia. But instead of breast tissue, there's just some extra skin and fat in the area. If this describes you, think about talking with a trusted adult or your doctor—there may be lifestyle changes (like eating differently and exercising more) that could help with this issue.

Chest Changes

The shape of your body will change during puberty. One of the most noticeable differences is in the chest. Your shoulders will broaden, and the muscles along your arms, chest, and back will grow. Your top half might start to look wider than your waist. Or not. Everyone's body is different.

What will happen for sure is that you will have a growth spurt and a strength spurt. And it happens in that order: First you will grow, and then you will get stronger. How you will be shaped is a combo of your genetic code and your lifestyle choices, including what you eat and drink and how you exercise.

WHERE'S my HAIR?

The sprouting of chest hair is as unpredictable as any other feature of puberty—it's definitely going to happen, but no one can say when. Some guys start to notice a few hairs in middle school, while others graduate from high school with hardly any at all. And chest hair is one of those things that continues to change as you get older, with most guys noticing that they grow a lot more hair in their 20s. Hair can grow on your nipples, too, as well as in the center of your chest and higher toward your neck.

the SECTION ABOUT

4

BELLY-ZONE

YOUR MIDDLE.

UNDERSTANDING SIZE
and SHAPE with LOTS ABOUT
SMART EATING and DRINKING

BELLY ZONE
49

SHAPES and SIZES

All bodies are different. All bodies are good.
There's no one right kind.

REALITY CHECK

Remember that lots of images of people aren't realistic at all. This is especially true for celebrities in magazines and online and in movies, but it's even true with your friends who use apps to alter their pictures. This goes for guys and girls alike. Many photos have been electronically altered so that a person looks completely different from how he actually appears in real life. So there's no great reason to compare yourself to anyone—not the guy sitting next to you in class, and not the actor in your favorite action movie, either.

All Different Shapes

You are who you are. And your features are what they are, too. You are born with a particular nose shape, eye color, hair texture, and skin tone. The same is true for your shape and size: Some guys are tall and lanky, while others are short and sturdy. Some kids will enter puberty early and change when they are younger, while others will be "late bloomers" and won't develop until they are older.

It's all normal, and, frankly, it's all pretty much out of your control. Most kids will have a body shape that is similar to someone else in their family. Your lifestyle choices matter, but your genetics matter, too. No one body type is better or worse than another—they're just different. What really matters is how you treat your body so that it can be fit and healthy.

All Different Sizes

Weight stresses a lot of people out. But it's important to know that there's no such thing as one ideal weight. A healthy weight depends on how tall someone is and how his body is proportioned. And things can shift pretty quickly during puberty, especially with a growth spurt. As guys start growing and changing, some get concerned about their weight. If you fit into this category, don't decide to go on a diet on your own. Talk to your parents or doctor first to find out if it's necessary. Then you can set weight and fitness goals based on what's healthiest for you and what makes sense for your particular body type.

Being the Big Guy

Kids who are taller or larger than average can be mistaken for being older. This might not sound like a big deal—in fact, to some, this seems pretty great. But for the guys who fall into this category, being treated as if they are older can be a burden or a challenge. Looking more mature can give others the sense that a guy is able to do certain things—from answering a question to scoring on a team— just because he looks older than he really is.

Even trickier, many people expect that older-looking kids can make more mature decisions. The truth is, looking older has nothing to do with maturity. If this describes you, do your best to take it in stride. It's also OK to share your age. People often appreciate knowing, and, more than that, they will probably be impressed by the maturity it takes to speak up.

Being the Little Guy

Some guys are just rail-thin, no matter what they do to try to beef up. Other guys are short and don't seem to grow at all even while everyone around them is sprouting up. It can be frustrating to be smaller—and to be seen as younger—but studies show that there can be benefits, too. Often, smaller boys will work harder at sports because they don't have the advantage of size. Practicing more and putting in 100% effort can bring huge rewards. Kids who do that tend to improve faster, and, once they do grow, they are even more of a force to be reckoned with.

WHERE'S my SIX-PACK?

One of the big shifts during puberty is an increase in muscle mass. But don't expect to suddenly see bulging biceps and six-pack abs when you look in the mirror. These changes take time. It's also important to know that the images of men all around you—in magazines, on TV, in the movies, and online—can make guys think that super-defined muscles are the norm. They aren't. Muscles appear when guys exercise regularly and eat healthfully. But they aren't necessarily a sign of health. If you are looking to have a muscular frame, you need to be careful about how you approach it. Get help from adults who know how to train people safely—intense workouts can be damaging if done without guidance, and weight lifting is usually not recommended for kids.

BELLY ZONE

DRINKS

Water is the only beverage you need. So drink up!

Your MVP: Water

Want to know the *only* drink your body really needs? Yep, water. That's because your body is about two-thirds water, and that water needs to be replenished regularly.

Water keeps you hydrated. When you drink sodas, juices, vitamin beverages, or special sports drinks—even when you are working out or playing hard—it's the water in those drinks that makes the difference. But water has no sugar, no artificial colors, no caffeine, no added chemicals. All those missing ingredients make water *pure perfection* for your body.

And you need to drink lots every day, especially during and after exercise. Milk is a great alternative, because it is packed with protein and calcium.

FUN PEE FACT:

How do you know if you have had enough water today? Take a look at your pee. If it is dark yellow, then you are not hydrated enough and you should think about guzzling a glass of water right now. If it is clearish-yellow, then you're doing great. The color will change throughout the day and night, so get into the habit of checking. This is really the easiest way to avoid dehydration.

PALE STRAW color: **GREAT!**

TRANSPARENT YELLOW: **ALSO OKAY!**

DARK YELLOW: **DRINK WATER SOON!**

HONEY COLOR: **DRINK WATER NOW!**

Sports Drinks

The first sports drink was invented in the 1960s by a Florida football coach who wanted to help rehydrate and energize his players during long, hot practices. The team name was the Florida Gators, so he called the drink Gatorade. The drink mixed sodium (salt), potassium, and phosphate with a little bit of sugar, some lemon juice, and water. This combination was designed to replace the water and electrolytes (natural salts in your blood) the athletes were sweating out. When the team won a championship that year, Gatorade got a lot of the credit. Today, sports drink recipes are pretty similar to the original Gatorade—but they often have a bunch more sugar and coloring added as well.

The thing is, even though you may run and play and sweat a ton, unless you are an elite athlete, you don't need a special drink to rehydrate. You just need water.

In fact, most sports and vitamin drinks today do more harm than good. They add tons of processed sugar to your diet—the average 20-ounce bottle contains 7–9 teaspoons in there. That's an entire day's worth of sugar in one bottle! So do yourself a favor and act like a real athlete who respects his body. This means that most of the time, you stick with water to hydrate.

Bodybuilding Beverages

Lots of drinks promise to make your muscles bigger and stronger. These beverages, available in many stores, tend to be advertised especially to boys and men. The drinks contain a bunch of vitamins, minerals, and proteins. Some have the word "milk" in their name, even though they may not contain any milk. Most doctors don't consider these drinks to be healthy. They have lots of protein, which can be hard for your kidneys to manage, and they often have many extra ingredients, too, such as artificial sweeteners and a long list of additivies. Bottom line? Bodybuilding drinks aren't meant for kids— even the companies that make them say so.

HOW MUCH SUGAR?

5 TEASPOONS of SUGAR

8 TEASPOONS of SUGAR

Are Smoothies Healthy?

Sort of. Some smoothies are definitely better than others. If it seems like anything that is made with fruit should be good for you, then it's time to think about this situation a little differently. Yes, fruit is great. It has natural sugar, which is a whole lot better for you than many other sweeteners. And fruit is packed with fiber, helping its sugar to be absorbed slowly. The fiber also fills you up when you eat fruit one piece at a time.

The problem with a smoothie is that you are putting lots of fruit together in a blender—much more than you would ever eat if it were cut up on a plate and served that way. Think about this: one banana + two apples + two oranges + half a pineapple + a few strawberries. That is MUCH more fruit than you could hold in your two hands, but it might blend up into a drink that you could suck down in a few minutes. That's a lot of sugar, even if it is the natural kind. Plus, by blending up the fruit, you are chopping up all the good fiber so it cannot do the job it is meant to do.

So what are the best smoothies?

Small. If you have a small smoothie, then you are drinking about as much fruit as you might actually eat.

Simple. Smoothies with ice cream or frozen yogurt added are basically just fruit-flavored milkshakes. Instead, stick to fruit-only smoothies with a splash of milk, fresh juice, or water added to help blend the fruit. You can also add some yogurt or a spoonful of nut butter for extra protein.

8 TEASPOONS of SUGAR

9 TEASPOONS of SUGAR

FOOD

Healthy eating habits give your body the fuel it needs to power through your day.

Eating a Balanced Diet

Some foods are good for you, and some foods aren't. This is not a news flash. The fact is that some foods—such as whole grains, lean proteins, fruits, and vegetables—have more nutrients than others. They make you feel more energetic by providing healthy fuel, so these are the foods that you should eat most of the time. But this doesn't mean that you can't enjoy treats. Foods that are higher in fat or sugar (desserts and snack foods such as chips) are OK occasionally. The key is *moderation*. That means not eating too much of anything. So here's your goal: Make your meals and snacks a mix of different kinds of foods. Eat lots of variety, and make most of it healthy.

Knowing When to Eat

Do:

- Eat when you are hungry or when it has been a few hours since you last ate.
- Go slowly, chew your food, use utensils, and put your fork down between bites.
- Stop when you are no longer hungry—this happens before you feel full.

Don't:

- Eat when you are bored, staring at a screen, or when some snack just happens to be available.
- Eat to deal with emotions such as nervousness, worry, or sadness.
- Just eat out of routine—there's no need to consume more if you are full, even if something really tasty is available.

Smart Snacks

Do you feel like you are starving in between meals? Most kids (and adults, too) can't go hours and hours without eating. Turns out that snacking is actually good for you because food is fuel, no matter what time of day you eat it. So think of snacks as mini-meals—grab healthy stuff such as fruit, raw veggies, cheese, yogurt, and whole-grain crackers spread with nut butter. Don't make snacking an excuse to eat junk.

Eating Vegetarian

Being vegetarian means that you don't eat meat. Vegetarians can get all the protein, vitamins, and minerals they need, but it takes a little extra effort—you can't just pass over the steak and fill up on fries and still be healthy.

Dictionary of Eating

carnivore: a person who eats meat

vegetarian: a person who doesn't eat any kind of meat, including fish

pescatarian: a vegetarian who does eat fish

vegan: a vegetarian who doesn't eat any animal products—so no eggs, honey, or dairy products, either

NUTRITION

Pack your meals and snacks with good food
to keep you healthy.

A Balancing Act

To eat right, you need to know which foods are good for
you and how much of them to eat at a time. It's actually
pretty easy.

- Make your plate colorful—have at least two or three
  colors on there.
- About half of your plate should have fruits and veggies.
- Notice what's *not* on there: high-sugar desserts. Sure,
  you can have them occasionally, but they shouldn't
  show up at every meal.

Grains, such as
- whole wheat
- oats
- brown rice
- wild rice

Fruits, such as
- bananas
- oranges
- raisins
- apples
- peaches
- pears

Dairy products, such as
- milk (cow, soy, almond—
  or any type you like best)
- yogurt
- cheese

FRUITS   GRAINS

VEGGIES   PROTEIN

Vegetables, such as
- spinach
- carrots
- broccoli
- kale
- sweet potatoes
- beets

Proteins, such as
- chicken or turkey
- beef
- nuts and nut butters
- fish
- tofu
- eggs

Don't Stuff Yourself!

You probably know what it's like to overeat—your stomach might hurt just thinking about it. How can you avoid doing that again? The best time to stop eating is when you are no longer hungry, and that happens before you are actually full. The feeling of fullness takes time.

So when you are eating at home:

Go slow: When you eat super fast, you won't feel full until it's way too late.

Go smart: Take a look at how much food you serve yourself. Think about portion size, and don't start with a crazy huge amount.

Go small: Try using smaller plates, cups, and even utensils.

And when you are eating away from home:

Sizing: Avoid ordering value-size meals at restaurants—they are usually huge! If you do order a large portion, share it or take home the extras.

Servings: Start looking at the "serving size" on labels. ••••▶ This is the amount that the manufacturer thinks is reasonable to eat or drink in one sitting. That amount can be different from how much is inside the package.

INSTEAD of... CHOOSE...

french fries,

popcorn sprinkled with Parmesan cheese.

a bowl of ice cream,

a glass of milk.

a bag of chips,

a handful of roasted almonds.

SERVING SIZE

Did you know?

- That 20-ounce sports drink that you guzzle down after a game is actually 2.5 servings.

- A bag of chips that looks like it's for one actually contains 1.5 servings.

- When you pour a bowl of cereal, you probably pour 2 to 3 servings.

Nutrition Facts

Serving Size 2/3 Cup (55g)
Servings Per Container 8

Amount per serving

Calories 230

	% Daily Value*
	00%
Total Fat 0g	5%
Saturated Fat 1g	
Trans Fat 0g	0%
Cholesterol 0mg	7%
Sodium 160mg	13%
Total Carbohydrate 37g	14%
Dietary Fiber 4g	
Total Sugars 12g	
Includes 10g Added Sugars	20%
Protein 3g	
	10%
Vitamin D 2mcg	20%
Calcium 260mg	45%
Iron 8mg	6%
Potassium 235mg	

* The % Daily Value (DV) tells you how much a nutrient in a serving of food contributes to a daily diet. 2,000 calories a day is used for general nutrition advice.

BELLY ZONE

What's a Whole Food?

A whole food is something that grew out of the ground or on a tree, or else it came from nature but isn't processed by machines. A whole food is not something that can live on a shelf for 10 years. In general, whole foods are better for you than processed ones.

Diet Foods

Here's a little-known fact: Diet foods that are sweetened with artificial sugars usually aren't much better for you than super sugary ones. Even though a diet soda has "zero calories," your body still has trouble digesting it. You are *much* better off with a naturally sweet food (such as fruit) than a diet cookie, candy, or drink.

Eating Disorders

Everyone needs to eat because food provides the fuel our bodies need to function. But some people struggle with how they think about food. When this happens, it is often connected to how they feel about their bodies. **Eating disorder** is the term used to describe an unhealthy relationship with food.

One type of eating disorder is **anorexia**, which is when a person severely restricts what he eats, usually in the hope of losing weight. Another eating disorder is **bulimia**, which is when a person eats but then "purges" or gets rid of the food he just ate by making himself throw up, exercising excessively to burn through the calories, or taking a medicine to make the food pass through his body quickly.

Eating disorders affect both boys and girls, and they can be dangerous. If you struggle with eating—or even if you are just confused about how to think about food—talk to a parent or your doctor.

Mindfulness and Body-fullness

Being a healthy eater is all about the big picture. You don't need to be perfect at every meal. The goal is to eat mostly healthy throughout the day. If you didn't have a great breakfast, give yourself a break and remember there's still lunch, dinner, and snacks where you can make better choices.

THE BIG PICTURE

VITAMINS

To power your body, choose a daily diet packed full of essential vitamins and minerals.

Vitamin A

What it does: Provides a boost for your immune system, which fights infection, and also helps your eyes, especially night vision

Where to find it: milk, eggs, orange and yellow vegetables (carrots, sweet potatoes, and squash), green leafy vegetables, and fruits like apricots, mangoes, and cantaloupe

Vitamin C

What it does: Helps to grow and repair tissues all over your body, including strong gums, bones, ligaments, and even skin and blood vessels. It also stimulates your immune system, so it helps healing and protects you from colds, too.

Where to find it: citrus fruits (oranges), strawberries, broccoli, peppers, spinach, and peas

Vitamin E

What it does: Helps to boost the immune system and protect cells all over the body from damage

Where to find it: oils (olive oil, sunflower oil and grapeseed oil), fish, sunflower seeds, leafy green vegetables, nuts (especially almonds and peanuts), and avocados

Vitamin D

What it does: Strengthens teeth and bones

Where to find it: milk, eggs, and salmon. The sun also helps here—when sunlight hits your skin, it helps your body make vitamin D. All you need is about 10–15 minutes of sun exposure a day to get the benefits.

The B Vitamins

What they do: Help convert food into fuel, giving you energy. Some of the B vitamins also help your nervous system function well and help in the production of red blood cells.

Where to find them: leafy green vegetables, beans, animal products (meat, fish, poultry, eggs, and dairy), and whole-grain products, especially fortified cereals, breads, pastas, and rice

Vitamin K

What it does: Essential for blood clotting so that you can stop bleeding when you're cut

Where to find it: green leafy vegetables such as kale, spinach, Swiss chard, romaine lettuce, and collard greens—the darker green, the better! Also in edamame, meat, and eggs

Calcium

What it does: Helps to develop strong teeth and bones and also aids muscle and nerve function

Where to find it: dairy products (yogurt, cheese, and milk), fish (particularly sardines and salmon), almonds, oranges, and dark leafy green veggies

Iron

What it does: Essential for the production of blood cells so that they can carry oxygen

Where to find it: meat (red meat, poultry, pork, and fish); dried fruits (apricots and raisins); beans, iron-fortified whole-grain breads, cereals, and pastas; and dark leafy greens

Do I Get Enough?

It's not always easy to get all the vitamins you need only from the food you eat, especially if you are a picky eater. Taking a multivitamin supplement can help fill in where your diet falls short. There are lots of choices in the vitamin aisle—pills or gummies to chew, or pills to swallow. A parent or doctor should help choose the best one for you.

BELLY ZONE

65

OTHERS ARE
SUPER PRIVATE...

like all the
CHANGES to
YOUR PRIVATES.

HORMONES

Hormones are natural chemicals. When puberty begins, it's like a giant science experiment is going on inside you, and that's when the changes start.

What's Gonna Happen?

Even though puberty itself can be pretty unpredict-able, once a part of the body starts changing, it usually changes in a predictable way. That means your genitals will develop in a certain way. And you will get hair in different places—first here, then there. And your voice will change by squeaking first, then dropping. All these different body parts develop when they are ready to; the way it happens for one guy is not necessarily the way it will happen for another. But once a certain part gets going, there is some predictability about what will happen next in that spot. That can be a relief.

Remember that the changes that happen to the body during puberty can start anytime between ages 9 and 14, and they happen slowly over years. Some boys are completely done growing and changing by age 14 or 15, but others don't finish until after high school. All of these guys are normal.

What is it?
Testosterone is a naturally produced chemical called a **hormone**. In general, a hormone is made in one part of your body and tells another part (or many parts) what to do.

Where does it come from?
Most of your testosterone is made in your testicles, but a tiny bit is also made in the adrenal glands that sit on top of your kidneys.

What does it do?
A lot. Testosterone gets the cred-it for helping to transform you from a boy into a man. But it also has many other jobs in the body. In fact, you will need testoster-one for the rest of your life—it's not just a puberty thing. **Here are some of the ways testosterone works in guys' bodies:**

PUBERTY is SNEAKY

PUBERTY

TESTOSTERONE

to TESTOSTERONE

Affects your moods, making them swing. Sometimes guys in the midst of puberty get super quiet and withdrawn. Other times they experience feelings of anger, frustration, or even rage. While these mood shifts are common during puberty and testosterone certainly plays a role, scientists still debate how closely moodiness and testosterone are linked.

Contributes to the growth of hair, including facial hair, pubic hair (that's hair "down there"), and eventually all-over body hair.

Stimulates growth of your larynx (voice box). It also makes changes in your vocal cords, which makes your voice deeper.

Grows your muscles. First, testosterone makes muscles bigger, and then it makes them stronger.

Tells your penis and testicles to grow. Testosterone is made in your testicles. As more is made, the testicles get bigger and bigger. Eventually, testosterone instructs your testicles to produce sperm.

Testosterone, a Natural Steroid

There are good steroids, and there are bad ones.

The good ones:

• Natural steroids that your body makes without you even knowing it, such as **adrenaline** (for when you need to run fast) and sex hormones such as **testosterone** that transform you during puberty

• Steroid medicines that can help reduce swelling in your body—for instance, when you have an asthma attack or a severe allergic reaction

The bad ones:

Anabolic steroids. These are the lab-created versions of testosterone that are used by some people trying to build strength or speed more quickly than they can with training alone. Some athletes use these drugs even though they can be dangerous and using them can get you kicked out of competition. Some undesirable side effects of anabolic steroids: big-time acne, stunted growth, shrunken testicles, enlarged breasts, and extreme moodiness or even rage.

THYROID
HORMONE

INSULIN

MELATONIN

Other Hormones

Do guys have "girl" hormones? Yes, indeed. And girls have "guy" hormones, too. Remember that hormones are just natural chemicals made by the body. There are actually lots of different hormones inside you, and some of them have absolutely nothing to do with puberty. For instance:

• **Thyroid hormone** is involved with how your cells use energy, and so it affects everything from how you grow to how your body uses food for fuel.

• **Melatonin** is a hormone that makes you sleepy at night.

• **Insulin** is the hormone that tells your cells to allow sugar inside so that they can use it for fuel—**diabetes** occurs when a person either doesn't have enough insulin or it doesn't work the way it should.

So hormones are nothing new for you. They aren't things that appear just during puberty; instead, they are at work inside every single person at all times. But the sex hormones are different. As you now know, **testosterone** tells your body to develop features that look more male. **Estrogen** and **progesterone** are the hormones that do similar work in female bodies. Still everyone has a little of everything—girls have some testosterone, and boys have some estrogen and progesterone.

PUBIC AREA

The area below your belly button goes through major changes during puberty.

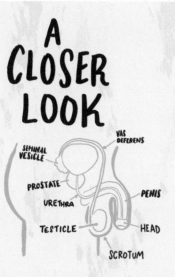

A CLOSER LOOK

SEMINAL VESICLE
VAS DEFERENS
PROSTATE
PENIS
URETHRA
TESTICLE
HEAD
SCROTUM

Circumcision

When a boy is born, the tip of his penis is covered by a piece of skin called the **foreskin.** Shortly after birth, some boys will have a circumcision, which means that this piece of skin is removed by a doctor or a trained religious figure. Parents choose to circumcise their sons based upon religious or cultural beliefs. While circumcised and uncircumcised penises look a little bit different, the only difference between a boy with foreskin and a boy without is how he cleans his penis in the bath or shower.

A Hairy Situation

Hormones made by the adrenal glands—little glands that sit on top of the kidneys—are called **adrenal androgens**. These hormones tell your body to start sprouting hair. Androgens don't actually cause puberty—that's testosterone's job—but levels of androgens and testosterone usually start rising around the same time. Emphasis on the word *usually*: This is why hair growth doesn't always sync up with the other changes in puberty.

Pubic Changes

Once you enter puberty, your penis and testicles will begin to grow and change, typically following a certain sequence.

Stage 1: What you look like before puberty starts. Testicles are small, penis is about the same size it has been for as long as you can remember, and there's no pubic hair.

Stage 2: Testicles start to grow, and the scrotum (the sac around the testicles) gets a little redder or darker, but the penis hasn't really grown yet. Maybe pubic hair begins to grow. At this stage, it is still thin.

Getting Kicked

If you get kicked or hit in the testicles, it's going to hurt. Like, SERIOUSLY hurt. So much that almost every guy who experiences it will double over in pain, and some even feel as if they are going to throw up or cry. Why does this happen? It's because the pain is felt in the scrotum, in the abdomen (your belly area), and in the head, too. There are direct—and very fast—nerve pathways in your body connecting your scrotum to these other parts. When the testicles get hit, messages are sent up to the brain screaming "Pain! PAIN!" Those particular signals are super strong, and the body gets the message extremely loud and clear. Messages are also sent to the nearby abdomen just because of the way your nerves are wired down in that part of the body.

Stage 3: Testicles grow more, and penis starts to grow. Now there's more hair, and it starts to become thicker and curlier.

Stage 4: Testicles still growing, and penis is, too. Skin covering the scrotum looks darker now. Hair down there is curly but still pretty much right around the base of the penis.

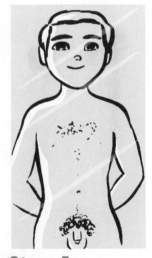

Stage 5: Testicles and penis have reached their adult size, and the pubic hair has spread out toward the thighs and up to the belly button.

BIG CHANGES

73

UNDERWEAR

When it comes to what you wear under your clothes, you've got some choices to make.

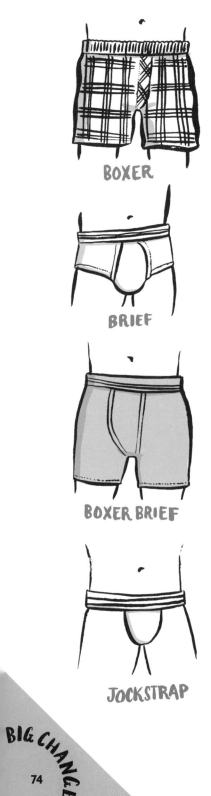

BOXER

BRIEF

BOXER BRIEF

JOCKSTRAP

Boxers vs. Briefs

Boxers are like lightweight shorts. Briefs hug your body tightly and resemble a diver's swimsuit. There are in-between styles, too, such as the hybrid boxer-brief. There is no one best type of underwear, so choose the kind you like. Regardless of style, pay attention to the material. Underwear made from natural fibers (such as cotton, bamboo, and silk) tend to be more breathable than underwear made from synthetic fibers (polyester or spandex).

Wear Your Underwear

There are several great reasons to always wear underwear and not go "commando," which means not wearing any! One reason? Zippers. Having a really sensitive part of your body get zipped accidentally will HURT, and it can also injure you. Also, some clothing fabrics (including jeans or denim) can irritate your skin. And because your underwear only gets one wear before it gets washed, it's just a lot cleaner to put that underwear layer between your body and your clothes.

What's a Jockstrap?

A jockstrap (also known as an athletic supporter) is designed to support your penis and testicles during sports. It literally straps everything down so that you can run and move without those body parts flapping around. Some jockstraps have a pouch to hold a cup, which is a plastic shield designed to protect your genitals if you get hit in the groin. Some types of underwear are designed to fit cups as well, so you may not have to wear a jockstrap if your sport requires protection down there.

It Smells Under There

Two things happen during puberty: You will sweat more than you used to, and you will sprout pubic hair. This combination can add up to some real stink, especially if you prefer wearing tighter-fitting underwear. It's totally normal, but it's also potent. So . . .

Wash up: Wash your groin thoroughly, using soap and water, every day in the shower. If you are not circumcised, it's important to wash beneath your foreskin. To do that, gently fold back the skin (never force it!), wash, rinse away all the soap, and then pull the foreskin back into place.

Dry up: Make sure to dry yourself really well after bathing. This includes underneath your scrotum, where the skin can stay damp unless you dry it with a towel.

Let 'em breathe: If you wear briefs, make sure to give your privates some breathing room overnight. Sleep in loose-fitting pajama bottoms or boxer shorts.

Change daily: There are lots of clothing items that can be reworn without washing—think jackets, sweaters, and jeans—but unless you have a clothing emergency, underwear is not on this list!

Try new kinds: Try different types of underwear to see if you sweat a little less down there. You can switch up the material or the fit. Synthetic materials, especially the ones used for athletic wear, can pull the sweat away from your body and trap it along with bacteria, so those garments can really reek after a while.

I'VE... SEEN THINGS.

TERRIBLE THINGS

REALLY DIRTY UNDERWEAR

Do you ever notice some brown marks in your underwear? Some people call them skid marks, like tire marks on a road. The difference? The marks in your underwear are made by poop. Pretty gross! There are really only a couple of ways those marks wind up in your underwear: either you're not wiping well enough after using the bathroom, or you're passing gas that accidentally includes a little bit of mess with it.

Do yourself and your parents a favor, since no one really likes to clean up messes like this: Take a little more time wiping after you poop. And if you are the kid who finds farting hilarious but you also find brown in your underwear at the end of the day, pick another way to crack yourself up.

ERECTIONS

This is a big change. When it starts happening, it might be surprising or even embarrassing. But it just means you're growing up.

What's Going On?

Your penis has always had the ability to change size and shape—ever since you were a baby. When it gets bigger and harder and sticks out away from your body, this is called an **erection.** And it's totally normal.

Erections are caused by blood filling up the tissue inside the penis. Even though the penis can get pretty hard, it's just blood and tissue in there (and no bone, despite nicknames for erections that you may have heard). There's no good answer for how long one might last—it's different for every guy. But the more it happens, the more you might be able to predict what's typical for you.

During puberty, you will start having more erections. It's just a fact of life. You can have them when you think about certain things or for no particular reason at all. You even have them several times during the night when you sleep. The worst is when an erection happens at the absolute wrong time—for example, when you're standing up in front of your class to give a presentation.

What's the Word?

There are lots of slang terms for body parts, particularly penises and erections. But using these words can be considered inappropriate and, in some situations, can get you into real trouble. That's why you should stick with the anatomical terms—the ones that doctors and parents and health teachers use. There's nothing "bad" about these words.

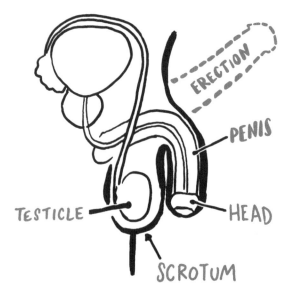

Ejaculation and Nocturnal Emissions

Here are some terms you need to know:

Sperm are made in the testicles and carry copies of your genes. If you ever have a baby, this is how those genes get passed along.

Semen is a mix of sperm from the testicles and fluid that is made near the testicles. It is whitish in color.

Ejaculation is when semen travels through the urethra and out the tip of the penis.

A wet dream—also called a **nocturnal emission**—is when semen comes out the tip of the urethra during sleep. This happens to almost all guys, some more than others. Like everything else with puberty, there's no exact age when you can expect it to occur. Wet dreams can feel really embarrassing because in the morning, there is a wet spot on the bed. Some guys worry that it's pee, but the spot doesn't smell like urine, and it's not yellow. If this happens to you, no biggie. Just think about cleaning up, especially if you don't want others to know. You can use a damp towel and wipe off the wet parts on the sheets. You can also take the sheet off your bed and put it in the laundry or else wash it yourself.

HIDING ERECTIONS

Since they sometimes happen when you least expect them, you might want to have a plan to manage surprise erections.

Excuse yourself: If you can, ask if you can be excused and go to the restroom or just take a short walk.

Distract yourself: Focusing on what's happening can make it worse. Try to think about *anything* else (a favorite vacation memory, a comic book you read, or some sports trivia). It might help your body settle down.

Cover yourself: Use your book bag or sweatshirt or whatever to cover your groin until the problem goes away. This can work if you're standing or sitting.

Lots of guys have erections when they wake up in the morning. To hide it from whoever else is in your room, roll over SLOWLY or keep your back to others.

SHAVING

You're going to grow hair on your face at some point.
If you decide to remove it, here's what to do.

Facial Hair

Just like everything else that happens during puberty, there is no exact "right" time to start shaving. That's because guys get facial hair at different ages. Regardless of when it starts to sprout, here's how it changes for most guys:

First: Thin hair will appear above your top lip—probably out by the sides at first. The hair is usually a little darker than the hair that was already there. (Yep! Your face is covered with hair and always has been—it's just so fine and light, you have probably never noticed it.)

Next: The hair gets thicker and darker and eventually spreads out over your entire mustache area. This might not happen for a year or two, or it could appear soon after you first notice fuzz on the corners of your upper lip.

Last: You'll sprout hair in the beard area, so that means on the cheeks, chin, and neck. But it usually doesn't grow in evenly at first—in fact, for many guys this takes years—so you'll probably have patches where there is hair growing and patches that look totally hairless.

When to Start Shaving

This is a totally personal choice. You shave when and if you want to. But you do need to involve a parent in this choice. You need an adult to walk you through how to shave before you put a blade up to your skin and go for it. It actually helps a lot if someone experienced stands there with you the first few times you shave.

Some guys start shaving as young as 10 or 11, and that's normal. If a fuzzy mustache feels annoying, then shaving might be appropriate. Some guys barely have to shave throughout high school—or they don't want to, or they're not allowed to. And that's normal, too.

HOW to SHAVE

1. Prep your skin:

Start by rinsing your face with warm water, or else shave right after you shower, when your skin is already damp and warm. Lather up the shaving cream, and spread it where you will shave. **Note:** Always use shaving cream or gel with blade razors. Some electric razors can be used with shaving cream, but others can't, so check out the details on the type you own.

2. Use the razor:

With most types of razors, shave downward along the mustache, cheeks, and sideburns, and then switch directions at the jawline, heading upward along the neck. The goal is to shave in the same direction that the hair is growing. **Note:** The direction of hair growth typically changes right at the jawline, but everyone's face is different.

3. Take care of the skin:

The best aftershave is just a cool water rinse followed by a pat dry, but some guys prefer special aftershave lotions, especially if their skin is sensitive. **Note:** Be careful with aftershaves. They can contain lots of perfumes and chemicals that can actually irritate the skin.

4. Clean up:

Rinse blade razors; brush out electric ones. **Note:** Don't forget to be considerate—rinse the sink and wipe the counter so that your tiny face hairs aren't scattered everywhere. The mess might not bother you, but everyone else who uses that bathroom will appreciate your cleaning up.

What's Razor Burn?

It's a rash on your face that HURTS. If you have it, your skin will sting and look red. It usually goes away after a day or two, but you can totally avoid getting razor burn in the first place: Don't use dull blades, and don't shave a dry face with a disposable razor.

What's an Ingrown Hair?

It's just what it sounds like: a hair that has grown inward. After you shave, most hairs grow back in the right direction (meaning, they poke out of your skin), but a few might get lost along the way. Hairs that cannot find the skin surface still grow, but they curl around themselves under the skin as they do. This is irritating, and so your body tries to fix it. An ingrown hair is similar to a pimple because your immune system sends cells to the area to fight the invader (in this case, the hair), and the skin on the surface can get red and can even develop a whitehead. Don't pick at an ingrown hair—it should go away on its own. If its really bothering you, check in with a parent.

RAZOR BURN

INGROWN HAIR

ELECTRIC vs. DISPOSABLE RAZORS

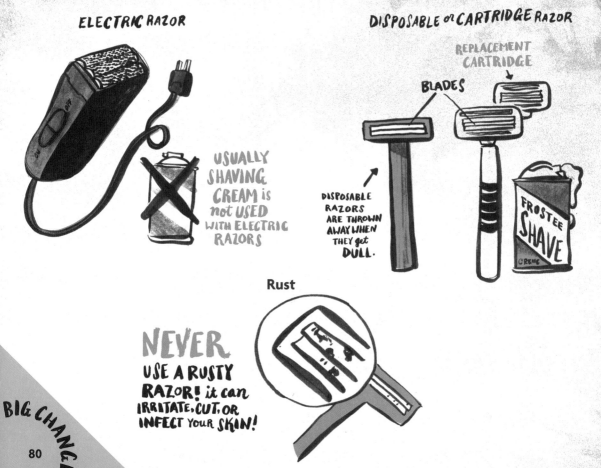

ELECTRIC RAZOR

USUALLY SHAVING CREAM is not USED WITH ELECTRIC RAZORS

DISPOSABLE or CARTRIDGE RAZOR

REPLACEMENT CARTRIDGE

BLADES

DISPOSABLE RAZORS ARE THROWN AWAY WHEN THEY get DULL.

FROSTEE SHAVE CREME

Rust

NEVER USE A RUSTY RAZOR! it can IRRITATE, CUT, OR INFECT YOUR SKIN!

Handling Nicks

What's the deal with the guy who has tiny pieces of tissue stuck to his face? Chances are, he cut himself shaving. It turns out, putting a small piece of toilet paper on the skin is a quick and easy way to stop the bleeding. But it's also easy to forget to take the paper off your face before you leave the house.

Other ways to fix a nick:

- Try rinsing your face with cold water or rub an ice cube against the skin for a few seconds. The cold makes blood vessels shrink instantly, which stops bleeding.
- Hot water can work, too. The heat cauterizes the skin, which means that it stops the bleeding thanks to a microscopic form of burning. (Don't worry—this is not really a burn!).
- Some people use astringents such as witch hazel. Astringents are products that cause the pores to constrict or tighten, which stops bleeding. They can really sting a cut, though.
- Other guys opt for petroleum jelly or lip balms. These work by putting a protective layer on the skin, helping to seal it.

the MYTH: HAIR GROWS back THICKER

Is It Thicker?!

Shaving doesn't make your hair grow back thicker, but it might look that way. That's because when you shave, you cut the hair straight across, and the blunt end looks bigger than the narrow, tapered end of an uncut hair.

VOICE

Sooner or later, your voice will start sounding different. Here's what to expect.

The Low-Down

There can be lots of ups and downs during puberty, and that includes your voice. By the time you are fully grown, you will have a deeper sound than the one you started with. But as with so many other parts of this process, you cannot predict exactly when this is going to happen for you or how obvious the change is going to be.

Here's what is going on: During puberty, the part of your throat that controls your voice, called your **larynx** (or voice box), will grow. The thin muscles that lay on top of the larynx—these are the **vocal cords** that actually make the sounds when you speak or sing or laugh or burp—stretch and thicken as well. These changes affect the way the vocal cords vibrate, and so they alter the way you sound. Longer, thicker cords make the voice sound deeper.

Why Does the Voice Crack?

Your voice—and actually most of the sounds you make—comes from air pushing up from your lungs and past your vocal cords, making the cords vibrate. As your larynx and vocal cords are shifting and growing, you may make weird high squeaks and low cracks. The whole process usually takes a few months (sometimes longer, sometimes shorter), and then your voice will settle into its new pitch without any more surprises.

What's That Lump?

Most guys start to notice a bump sticking out from the middle of their neck, a couple of inches below their chin. That's the **larynx.** When it grows, it becomes more visible on guys. Lots of people call this the Adam's apple.

MOODS

It's not just your body that's changing.
Puberty can make you *feel* different, too.

The Downs and Outs of Puberty

Puberty isn't just about body changes. It can feel like an emotional roller coaster, too.

Boy moodiness generally falls into two categories:
- Quiet and withdrawn, or
- Angry, impulsive, or aggressive.

Now, this isn't true for every guy—not at all! Some guys stay pretty even-keel, and they don't get very outwardly emotional. You may be the mellowest person you know. But in general, many guys experience the feeling of wanting to totally disappear at some point during puberty, and they also describe feeling the exact opposite—wanting to aggressively jump into the middle of something. Both are often overreactions to the reality of a situation.

Of course, many guys do more than just retreat into themselves or act out. Some will act silly or whiny or flustered. Some will be super dramatic. Emotions look different on different people. Simple as that.

But why these emotional swings? Partly because of testosterone, which is zinging around your body like crazy during puberty. Emotional reactions aren't ruled entirely by hormones, though. They have a lot to do with your personality, your life circumstances, and the particular situation you are reacting to. Every person is allowed to feel all these different ways.

How to Boost Your Mood

Pretty much all kids will say that they don't like how it feels to be emotionally out of control. They prefer being calm, cool, and collected—or at least feeling like themselves. So how can you become the master of your own emotions? Here are some simple tricks:

Don't stress out. Take some time for yourself when you need it.

Sleep! This resets your mood big-time, especially if you get a good night's sleep regularly.

Think ahead. How should you react in a certain situation?

Count to 10. In the heat of the moment, this lets you cool off.

Treat your body well. Do this by eating healthy foods and exercising regularly. These things actually make you feel happier.

Apologize. This will help you feel better if you've done something you regret.

Give yourself a break. Made a mistake? It's not the end of the world. You are a kid, and no one expects you to be perfect. Just work to do things differently next time.

Your LEGS and FEET will DEFINITELY GROW...

6 GET GOING

and MIGHT even ACHE.

HOW to **EXERCISE**
when to **BACK** off...
WHY you **NEED** to **SLEEP**

LEGS and HEIGHT

Your legs are about to get longer and stronger and hairier.

Growth Spurt

Oh yeah, you are going to get taller. Kids grow an average of 2 inches per year, every single year. That's an average, so some years you'll grow more than that and some years less. When you have your growth spurt, you will grow 3 to 4 inches per year, and this could last two or even three years! That means anywhere from 6 to 12 inches of new height over a pretty short period of time. Growth spurts happen at different ages for different boys—usually anytime between ages 10 and 16, and sometimes even into your late teens.

Ladies First?

Girls tend to have their growth spurts at younger ages than boys. This explains why the average middle school girl is taller than the average middle school boy. But remember, not everyone follows this rule, and every single kid goes at the pace that's right for him.

Sleep . . . and Grow

This is cool: You grow while you sleep. This has to do with the way growth hormone is released into your body when you are snoozing. So if you are in the middle of a growth spurt, you might be exhausted—that's a real thing. Best solution? Sleep it off . . . and grow even more.

Growing Pains

When the legs get longer, it can actually hurt. This is particularly true when you are growing fast and your legs feel tired, achy, even cramped. Usually, when kids realize that they are hurting because they are growing, they don't mind so much.

Leg Hair

About the time you start to grow hair under your arms, you may notice that you're sprouting more hair on your legs, too. Eventually, you'll grow hair lots of places. Your arm hair will thicken, and you'll get some on your chest. Body hair sometimes feels especially noticeable because it can grow in looking pretty dark.

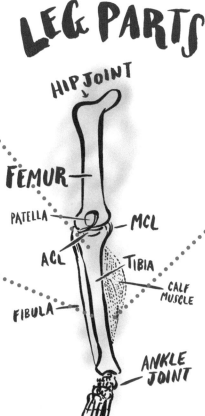

LEG PARTS

Osgood-Schlatter point: The spot near the top of the tibia where the tendon (the connection between muscle and bone) inserts. This area can become swollen and painful if the tendon pulls on the top layer of the bone as you grow.

Shin-splint site: The point of tenderness at the front of the tibia, about halfway down the lower leg. Pain here is associated with sports and new activities.

Charley horse spot: Squeezing and burning of the muscle as a result of spasm—that means that the muscle cannot stop contracting. This happens most often in the leg or foot, and it can feel as if your muscle is stuck in one position.

HIP JOINT

FEMUR

PATELLA

MCL

ACL

TIBIA

CALF MUSCLE

FIBULA

ANKLE JOINT

FEET

Your feet take a lot of pounding. Don't let foot and toe woes keep you sidelined.

Foot Odor

Your feet might stink. It's because feet sweat a lot, especially once you enter puberty. The best way to deal with foot odor is to prevent it. Here are some tips that will save you serious stench:

- Wear socks when you wear close-toed shoes—the socks will absorb sweat and draw it away from your skin.
- When socks look gross or smell stinky, trade them for a fresh pair.
- Wear shoes made of natural materials such as leather or canvas rather than plastic or fleece.

Ouch! Blisters

These sore spots form where your shoes rub against your skin, making a bubble that can pop or tear open. Sometimes this happens when shoes are too small or tight in one area. Keep your hands off! Most blisters heal better when left alone. You can put a bandage over a blister to protect it during the day, but remove the bandage at night to air it out and speed healing.

Itchy Fungus

Fungus loves to grow in dark, damp places. That's why it likes the little caves between your toes. Fungus can make your skin peel and feel itchy. It's called athlete's foot, but you don't need to be an athlete to get it. To fix it:

- Let feet breathe. Fungi don't like to grow in bright and breezy places, so wear open-toed shoes when you can. And at the end of every day, take off your shoes and socks to air out your feet.
- Wash and dry. In the shower, make an extra effort to wash (with soap), and when you get out, dry well in between all your toes.
- Air 'em out. Air dries sweat so if you wear flip flops or other open-toed shoes, the sweat (and the stink) won't accumulate in the first place.
- Try a treatment. There are lots of creams, powders, and sprays to help treat athlete's foot if airing out isn't enough to fix it.

On Your Toes

Got dirt? Wash it out! Use a nailbrush to clean beneath the nails.

And keep your nails short by trimming them regularly. This is easiest after showering or bathing because the nails are soft and easier to cut.

Toenail Care

Use a toenail clipper to clip straight across, short but not so short that it hurts. That way, you'll prevent painful ingrown toenails, which occur when a sharp corner of the nail continues growing and cuts its way into the skin around the nail.

Stinky Shoes

If your shoes reek, sprinkle baking soda or a shoe deodorizer in them, and let it sit overnight. Then shake out the baking soda—and the smell—in the morning by holding your shoes upside down over a trash can and gently knocking them together so the baking soda comes out. Reusable deodorizers that you drop into shoes can work great, too.

GET GOING

91

FITNESS

No matter what activity you do—soccer or swimming, kickball or karate—find a fun way to stay fit.

Active = Healthy

Regular exercise is key to making you look and feel awesome because it . . .
• Strengthens your muscles.
• Increases your flexibility.
• Reduces your stress.
• Improves your heart function and immune system.
• Builds your confidence.

If you are having one of those days when you feel super lazy, try remembering how amazing it feels to be active. Just get up and move!

It Adds Up

Things you can do during the day to get more exercise:
• Take the stairs instead of the escalator or elevator.
• Skip the ride when you only have to travel a few blocks. Walk instead.
• Ride your bike to a friend's house.
• Volunteer for muscle-building chores, such as weeding the garden or raking leaves.
• Turn off the video game and go play tag instead.
• Take the dog for a long walk or a run.

How Much Is Enough?

You need at least one hour of physical activity every day. This means doing just about anything that gets your muscles working, your heart rate up, and your lungs breathing faster.

You don't have to work out for one hour straight—you can break it up throughout the day. But you do need to push yourself. If you can sing or whistle a tune in the middle of your activity, then you should work out a little harder.

SPORTS SAFETY

Even the best athletes can get injured if they're not careful. So play it smart!

Warm Up, Cool Down

Every workout needs to involve stretching. A good warm-up prevents muscle pulls and tears. Cooling down at the end with more stretching reduces stiffness and soreness the next day and increases your overall flexibility, which is important for moving well in sports. All great athletes make time to warm up and cool down.

Wear the Right Gear

Depending on your sport, you need to be prepared and protected. When in doubt, wear the safety gear!

- Helmet to protect your head from scrapes, your skull from breaks, and your brain from concussion.
- Pads for elbows, wrists, and knees—they're way more comfortable than a cast.
- Bright clothes so that others can see you coming, especially when they're in cars.
- Well-fitting shoes and clothes to avoid unnecessary trips, falls, sprains, twists, blisters, and burns.

Don't Overdo It

Here's some advice that's super important: Pay attention to how your body feels while you're exercising or playing a sport. If you are in pain, or are dizzy, sick to your stomach, or unable to catch your breath, stop immediately and rest. These are warning signs to slow down and give your body a break.

Drink LOTS of Water

When you're working out, you need to hydrate. Your body keeps you cool by sweating, and you need to replace these fluids. It's easy: drink water before, during, and after you exercise. Bring a water bottle with you and refill it often.

S-T-R-E-T-C-H

Here's the deal with stretching: If you want to be both strong and flexible, you've got to do it. How?

- Stretch slowly. Ease your muscles carefully into or out of your workout—that takes time.
- Don't bounce. Once you strike your stretching position, hold the pose and sink deeper into it while you breathe.
- Hold it! Try to hold your stretch for a count of at least 10 to be sure your muscles get the message.
- Stretch both sides. One side is almost always easier to stretch than the other, so work through the tougher side.

GET GOING

94

Concussion Facts

A concussion is basically a bruise inside the brain. It acts like any other bruise on your body—the area swells a little and gets tender, and it takes time for it to heal.

So what's the big deal? If a concussion is just a bruise, why does everyone freak out about it? Because the bruise is in your brain, the control center of your body. Your brain doesn't heal as quickly or easily as other parts of your body. Healing from a concussion isn't like having a broken leg and being able to hobble around on crutches.

Concussions take time to get better. After a while, the swelling goes down. But if you keep reinjuring any bruise, it will only hurt more and stick around longer. This is why you need to rest your brain. Stimulating your brain when you have a concussion is no different than banging your leg against a chair when you have a huge bruise on your shin—it hurts, and it won't heal.

Concussion Rules

All concussions are different, and symptoms can include headache, confusion, lack of coordination, nausea, and sleepiness. Ask a parent to help you look up all the signs and become familar with them.

When in doubt, sit it out. Never go back to a game when you think you have a concussion.

Brain rest means that you shouldn't do anything to over-stimulate your brain. Talk to your doctor, but stay off screens and out of sports until your brain is healed.

When to Back Off

- If you are working out to the point of hurting yourself, you might be causing long-term harm to yourself.
- If you are injured, heal before you return to play.
- If you are exercising so hard that you cannot eat enough to keep up with what you are burning off, it's time to check in with someone about your routine.
- Remember that you are aiming to build lifelong fitness habits, and you don't need to become a world-class superstar right this second.

Sprain Training

Almost all athletes get injured. The most common injury is a sprain, which is a painful pull or tear inside a joint that causes it to swell or even turn black and blue. Any extremity can be sprained: fingers, wrists, elbows, knees, ankles, and toes. The best first way to manage a sprain is with RICE.

R - Rest, which means take a break and avoid using or putting weight on the sprained joint.

I - Ice packs (or bags of frozen veggies) help shrink swelling and ease the pain.

C - Compression means wrapping the sprained area snugly in a stretchy sports bandage. This keeps the joint stiff and protects it from further injury.

E - Elevate the sprained joint by propping it up. This reduces swelling.

If you are in a lot of pain or not getting better, then get to a doctor to have it checked out.

REST

Sleep is your body's way of recharging and rebuilding.
So get to it!

Good Night!
Here's what happens when you sleep:
• Your body grows.
• Your brain files away memories into long-term storage so that you can remember things better.
• Your mood is reset so that you feel rested and refreshed.

None of that happens with just 10 minutes of sleep. To get these benefits, you need a good night's sleep every night. And that can be tough to get.

How to Sleep
Watch the clock. Get up in the morning and go to bed at night around the same time every day, at least during the school week. Try to keep the schedule even on weekends, because if you sleep late one morning and then get up early the next, you may feel tired and groggy all day and have trouble sleeping that night.
Develop a routine before bed. This tells your body that it's time to go to sleep. Wash your face, brush your teeth, floss, and then get into bed and read or listen to music or write in a journal. Try to repeat this pattern every night around the same time.
Exercise. No kidding, exercise during the day really helps sleep at night. But some people can't exercise too close to bedtime or they have trouble winding down.
Watch what you drink, especially in the evening. Stay away from caffeine, which is found in lots of sodas, teas, coffee, and chocolate, too. It can make you feel jumpy and wide awake.
Shut down screens at least an hour (better yet, two hours) before bed. The light from the screen tells your brain to wake up, and this can really mess with your body's internal clock.

Melatonin

This is another hormone that your body makes naturally. Melatonin tells you to get tired so that you can fall asleep. Unfortunately, the light from screens on computers, tablets, and phones often interferes with melatonin. This means that when your brain wants to release melatonin in the evening to cue you that it's time for bed, your devices block that from happening. What's the big deal? Well, you may wind up staying awake much longer than you should. So let your melatonin do its job and power down all screens early in the evening.

How Many ZZZs?

Most kids need around 10 hours of sleep per night. Every night. This is different for everyone—some need less sleep and some need more. But many studies show that ten hours is pretty ideal for growing kids. If you have a few late nights in a row and you're exhausted, it's good to catch up on the weekend by going to bed early, sleeping in, or even napping.

But Adults Are Staying Up!

Is the sleep rule the same for adults? Yes and no. Adults don't need quite as much sleep as teens and tweens—they do pretty well with eight or nine hours. But that's more than many of them actually get. One reason adults don't need as much sleep is that they aren't growing. But otherwise, everything about sleep is the same for them as it is for you. When your parents have a good sleep routine, they are less crabby the next day, and their memory works better, too. Just like yours.

SLEEP TROUBLE

Lots of guys have problems that creep into their sleep.

Bed-Wetting

Peeing in bed while you are asleep can happen when your **bladder** (that's the sac that stores your urine) is too small or too weak to hold it all night. The medical name for bed-wetting is **enuresis**, and it's more common than you might think.

Some people wet the bed because they are super-deep sleepers and simply don't wake up when they need to go. Others have a bladder that needs to learn how to hold the pee a little better. But the good news is that almost everyone with enuresis outgrows it eventually. And most kids who have it find out that one of their parents did, too.

This is definitely something to talk about with your doctor. There are lots of treatments you can try—from alarms that help you wake up to prescription medicines that decrease the amount of urine your body produces at night. Habits can help, too: If you take breaks to go to the bathroom during the day, you are less likely to need to pee at night.

Insomnia

Insomnia is a medical word for not being able to sleep. There are tons of reasons why you might have a hard time sleeping such as:

• You might have a lot on your mind.
• You may be so excited or worried about something that you can't stop thinking about it.
• You might have had caffeine, which is an ingredient in some foods (chocolate) and drinks (coffee, tea, soda) that keeps you awake.
• You might have stayed on screens late into the evening.

Almost everyone has insomnia once in a while, but if you find yourself wide awake night after night, talk to a parent or your doctor. In the meantime, try this relaxation trick. Close your eyes and lie on your back. Then, SLOWLY, relax your feet, relax your legs, and keep going until you've relaxed every muscle in your body. From toe to head, you'll be ready to go—straight to sleep, that is!

Nightmares

It's completely normal to have a bad dream every once in a while. But that doesn't make them any less freaky. Nightmares can seem very real or totally absurd. The thing is, nightmares are often related to something that's actually bothering you. So if scary dreams invade your sleep every night, talk to your parents or a counselor to help you figure out what's really on your mind.

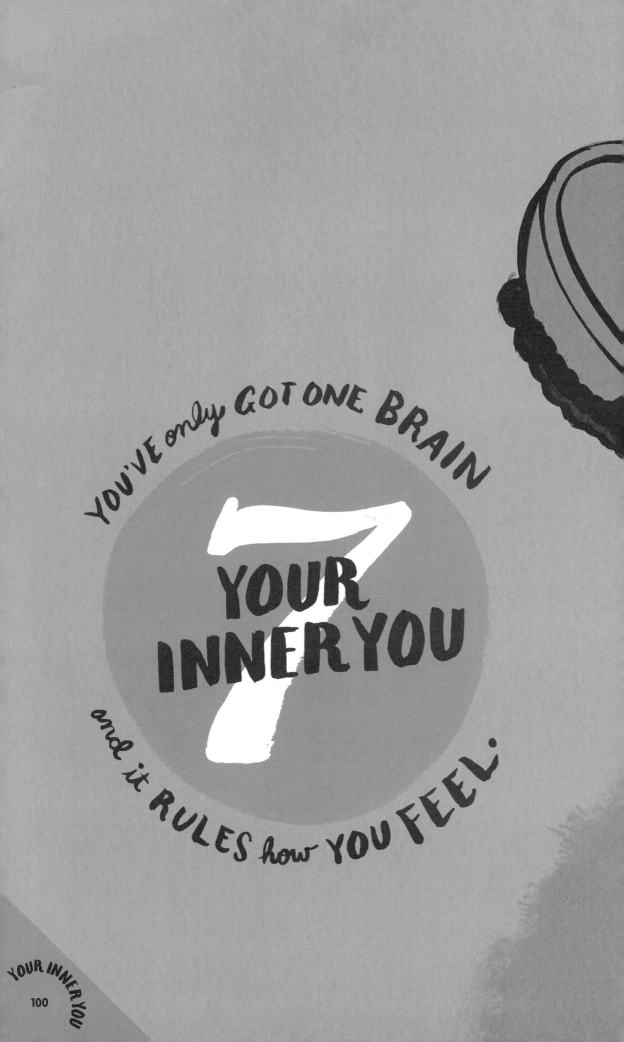

YOU'VE only GOT ONE BRAIN

7
YOUR INNER YOU

and it RULES how YOU FEEL.

HOW to KNOW YOURSELF, make SMART CHOICES and STAY CALM and COOL.

YOUR FEELINGS

Mad one minute, and sad the next? You're not going crazy—you're growing up.

Keep Out!

Feel like you want more privacy? That's totally fair. Most kids start to want privacy when they head into puberty.

But give your parents and siblings a break here. Resist slamming the door in their faces. Don't cut them out of your life if all you want is a little peace and quiet while you get changed. Having private moments to think or listen to music or talk to friends is important, but staying connected to your family is equally important. They love you. They look out for you. They want the best for you. And they're the people you can go to if your friends let you down. So find the balance between shutting the door and shutting people out.

Ups and Downs

At this point, you're pretty prepped for all the physical changes of puberty, but you may not be so sure about the emotional ones.

During puberty, your moods and opinions will change. A lot. Some days you'll feel like you are on top of the world, and other days you'll be down in the dumps. These feelings can even change from minute to minute. Can you guess what to blame? Yep, hormones. The same hormones that tell your body to develop can impact your feelings, too. Well, at least partly.

Other things affect your feelings as well. School life and home life are the biggies. There's a lot going on at school—between schoolwork, sports, clubs, and friends, something is bound to lift you up or get you down pretty much every day. And at home, now that you're older, you may be more aware of the way people in your house treat one another, or you may have responsibilities that feel like a burden. Everything going on inside you and around you changes how you feel, react, and even behave.

New Directions

It's great to get better and better at something you have done for a while. But you will also find yourself developing new interests as you get older. You might try something—a sport, class, or hobby—that you never considered before and love it. You may also begin to notice other kids in a more romantic way. That's normal. As you go through puberty, your life will fill up with a bunch of new feelings and experiences. It's one of the best things about this time in your life.

THE ENDOCRINE SOUND SYSTEM X

CANDY SAYS

THE GOGOS

Peer Pressure

A peer is a friend. Pressure is the feeling of being pushed. So peer pressure is the sense of being pushed by a friend. Peer pressure can be good or bad.

Positive peer pressure is a great thing, like when a friend motivates you to study for a test or do community service.

Negative peer pressure is what you want to stay away from. That's when a "friend" encourages or even bullies you into doing something you don't want to do. It could be something that's bad for you (like smoking), dangerous (like jumping off a roof), illegal (like shoplifting), or something that's fine but that you just don't feel like doing. That so-called friend is not acting much like a true friend at all.

FOLLOWING THE CROWD

It can be really hard to say no, especially if a bunch of people are doing the thing you want to get out of. Here's an important piece of advice: Don't lose your resolve. You are in charge of yourself, and you know what's right for you. Stick to that. It will be tough sometimes, but you can do it.

Some guys struggle with following their own path. You may wonder if you should try the new video game that everyone is talking about, even though you would rather spend your free time drawing or building or reading. This feeling is legitimately confusing, but don't just go along with the crowd. Sure, it's good to try something new every once in a while, but there's nothing wrong with sticking to what you know you're into. If some of your friends have moved on, you'll meet new ones who share your interests soon enough.

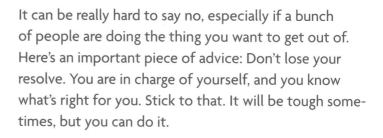

YOUR OWN WAY

Bullying

Bullying is being mean to someone (in person or online) over and over again, in a way that makes the person doing the bullying feel powerful.

Bullying is repeatedly talking about hurting someone, spreading rumors about someone, attacking someone physically or with words, or leaving someone out of a group on purpose.

Here are two big reasons people bully others:
• They care too much about popularity and want to hold onto or build up their social power.
• They are depressed or anxious, have low self-esteem, or don't feel connected to others.

If you SEE BULLYING happen, speak up. Tell the person doing the bullying to quit it. Be kind to the person being bullied. Or talk to a trusted adult about what you've seen.

If you are BEING BULLIED, humor can work great—just laugh off whatever the bully is doing. Or tell the bully, in a calm, clear voice, to STOP what he's doing. Do this every time. Sometimes you can stop bullying on your own. Or you might need a hand. Don't ever hesitate to tell a trusted adult what's happening.

If you are ACTING LIKE A BULLY, stop and think. Bullying behavior isn't just mean—it can have major consequences. Talk to a trusted adult to figure out what's making you feel like acting this way.

Time Out!

Think back to a time you've seen a kid have a full-on temper tantrum. Not pretty.

There are moments when we all feel like melting down, but hopefully you know by now that tears and screaming won't get you what you want, and you're learning how to control your emotions. A big part of growing up is learning how to express yourself calmly, even if you are furious. It's more fair to everyone around you, and, frankly, it's more likely to get you what you want.

Dealing with Feelings

Feelings come in a ton of different flavors: mad, sad, happy, silly, jealous, frustrated, embarrassed, and confused, to name just a few. Our feelings shift constantly throughout the day. That's totally normal.

But no one likes feeling emotionally out of control. We're used to flipping from excited to stressed or from bummed out to psyched, but if any one of these emotions is exaggerated, it feels bad. Screaming at someone you care about might make you feel as awful as he feels. So what can you do when emotion takes over and you are behaving, uh, not well?

1. **ID the problem.** You are allowed to have whatever feelings you have, but you need to figure out what's going on with you so that you can chill out a little. Think about how you're feeling and what happened to make you feel that way. Pay attention to your body, too—are your teeth clenched? Do you feel sick or tired or like you want to cry or punch something? All these things can be clues to help you solve the problem.

2. **Don't put up a wall.** If you give someone the silent treatment or if you yell at him, you have put up a barrier between yourself and that other person. Find a way to express how you feel so that you can resolve the problem. Share how you feel, and apologize when you have done something you know is hurtful.

3. **Smooth the road.** Make an extra effort next time around to do things a little differently. Every relationship can withstand bumps as long as you are willing to put in the work to fix them.

Cooling Down

OK, so you are mad. REALLY MAD. Before sharing your feelings, calm down. Breathe. Go for a walk or a run. Chill out. Write or draw. Hang out with your dog. Blow off that steam before you confront the person who made you so angry, and you'll be less likely to say or do something that you'll regret later. But then, once you've cooled off a bit, talk it out.

Talking It Out

It's important to tell people how you feel, honestly and calmly. This is huge in a relationship—it shows people how much you care about them and trust them. This advice applies to friends, parents, siblings, and anyone else who's important in your life.

Talking things through can help you figure out how you feel or what you should do in a particular situation. Plus, if you talk openly with someone you trust, that person will likely do the same right back. Think about it: Maybe that person needed someone to open up to, and you were the one who made him comfortable enough to do it. That's pretty cool.

Write It Down

If you don't have someone to talk to right away, or if you just aren't ready to talk yet, try writing in a private journal. This really works. In a journal, you can say whatever you want, however you want, to whomever you want. Organizing your feelings on paper can help you deal with them. And when you clear the junk out of your mind, you're making room for good stuff to take its place.

HOW and WHEN to TALK

DO!

Tell the person that you have something important to say. Clue him in that you are not being goofy.

Write down some notes if you are worried that you might forget everything you want to share.

Describe exactly how you feel. Say "I'm mad" or "I'm sad" or "I'm frustrated," and give a specific example about what happened.

Listen to what the other person has to say.

DON'T!

Start to share something major when you (or the other person) has somewhere else to be.

Interrupt one conversation because you think yours is more important.

Start by yelling. If you haven't calmed down yet, you aren't ready to talk.

BEING A GUY

When you're a guy, there are a lot of expectations about how you should be. They're not always right, though.

"Man-Up!"

Being a guy is tricky. On the one hand, you experience all sorts of emotions—this isn't just normal, it's healthy. But on the other hand, the world sends you lots of messages about *not* being this way. When a man is called "tough," it's usually meant as a compliment. The idea that boys and men shouldn't express their emotions is called "manning-up." But there's nothing manly about holding in your feelings.

It's important for people to keep their feelings in check. Freaking out about things usually isn't productive. But still, hang on to your emotions—don't ignore them or let them slip away. You absolutely can and should feel happy, sad, angry, proud, and everything in between. Becoming a man does not mean becoming someone who no longer expresses how he feels.

Boys Do Cry

They do. Every guy has done it. Boys cry for all kinds of reasons. They get physically or emotionally hurt. They get frustrated or angry or scared or sad or overwhelmed with happiness, and then tears come. Crying is nothing to be ashamed of. It means that you care, and that's a good thing.

There are times, though, when crying won't help a situation or you really want to avoid it. To keep your tears in check, try:
• Taking some deep breaths
• Swallowing a few times
• Yawning to relax your jaw
• Clearing your throat
• Taking a sip of water
Then let the tears out later if you still need to.

They're Called Feelings, So Feel Them

By now you know that emotions are normal. Actually, they are better than normal—they are amazing. Being able to feel pure joy is one of the great things about being human. Feeling anything, actually, is a gift. It means that you're living your life and experiencing everything that the world has to offer. Sure, it might be easier (and less painful) to avoid the downs in life, but if you never felt the downs, you wouldn't feel the ups, either.

You are who you are, which is exactly who you are supposed to be. And you are awesome. Really own that feeling, just like all the others.

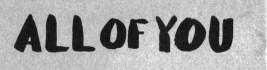
ALL OF YOU

You've learned a lot of important guy stuff in this book. But remember that there's more—much more—to you than just the body you've got. It's your heart, your mind, and your spirit that make you YOU.

EYES
For seeing things in your own way

EARS
For hearing ideas and other points of view

ARMS
For high-fiving and back-patting

LEGS
For standing up for what's right

HEAD
For figuring out how to make stuff happen

VOICE
For expressing what you think and what you want

HEART
For powering your dreams and goals

FEET
For moving ahead toward whatever future you choose

Write to us!

We love hearing from boys just like you. Tell us what you think of *Guy Stuff: The Body Book for Boys*. Send your thoughts and questions to:

Guy Stuff Editor
8400 Fairway Place
Middleton, WI 53562

(All comments and suggestions received may be used without compensation or acknowledgment. Sorry—photos can't be returned.)